Humility

~ ※ ~

By *Andrew Murray*

Lord Jesus! may our Holiness be perfect Humility!
Let Thy perfect Humility be our Holiness!

TABLE OF CONTENTS

PREFACE 3

HUMILITY: THE BEAUTY OF HOLINESS 4

HUMILITY: THE GLORY OF THE CREATURE 4

HUMILITY: THE SECRET OF REDEMPTION 6

HUMILITY IN THE LIFE OF JESUS 8

HUMILITY IN THE TEACHING OF JESUS 9

HUMILITY IN THE DISCIPLES OF JESUS 11

HUMILITY IN DAILY LIFE 12

HUMILITY AND HOLINESS 14

HUMILITY AND SIN 16

HUMILITY AND FAITH 18

HUMILITY AND DEATH TO SELF 19

HUMILITY AND HAPPINESS. 21

HUMILITY AND EXALTATION 23

ENDNOTE 25

A PRAYER FOR HUMILITY 25

Preface

There are three great motives that urge us to humility. It becomes me as a creature, as a sinner, as a saint. The first we see in the heavenly hosts, in unfallen man, in Jesus as Son of Man. The second appeals to us in our fallen state, and points out the only way through which we can return to our right place as creatures. In the third we have the mystery of grace, which teaches us that, as we lose ourselves in the overwhelming greatness of redeeming love, humility becomes to us the consummation of everlasting blessedness and adoration.

In our ordinary religious teaching, the second aspect has been too exclusively put in the foreground, so that some have even gone to the extreme of saying that we must keep sinning if we are indeed to keep humble. Others again have thought that the strength of self-condemnation is the secret of humility. And the Christian life has suffered loss, where believers have not been distinctly guided to see that, even in our relation as creatures, nothing is more natural and beautiful and blessed than to be nothing, that God may be all; or where it has not been made clear that it is not sin that humbles most, but grace, and that it is the soul, led through its sinfulness to be occupied with God in His wonderful glory as God, as Creator and Redeemer, that will truly take the lowest place before Him.

In these meditations I have, for more than one reason, almost exclusively directed attention to the humility that becomes us as creatures. It is not only that the connection between humility and sin is so abundantly set forth in all our religious teaching, but because I believe that for the fullness of the Christian life it is indispensable that prominence be given to the other aspect. If Jesus is indeed to be our example in His lowliness, we need to understand the principles in which it was rooted, and in which we find the common ground on which we stand with Him, and in which our likeness to Him is to be attained. If we are indeed to be humble, not only before God but towards men, if humility is to be our joy, we must see that it is not only the mark of shame, because of sin, but, apart from all sin, a being clothed upon with the very beauty and blessedness of heaven and of Jesus. We shall see that just as Jesus found His glory in taking the form of a servant, so when He said to us, 'Whosoever would be first among you, shall be your servant,' He simply taught us the blessed truth that there is nothing so divine and heavenly as being the servant and helper of all. The faithful servant, who recognizes his position, finds a real pleasure in supplying the wants of the master or his guests. When we see that humility is something infinitely deeper than contrition, and accept it as our participation in the life of Jesus, we shall begin to learn that it is our true nobility, and that to prove it in being servants of all is the highest fulfilment of our destiny, as men created in the image of God.

When I look back upon my own religious experience, or round upon the Church of Christ in the world, I stand amazed at the thought of how little humility is sought after as the distinguishing feature of the discipleship of Jesus. In preaching and living, in the daily intercourse of the home and social life, in the more special fellowship with Christians, in the direction and performance of work for Christ, —alas! how much proof there is that humility is not esteemed the cardinal virtue, the only root from which the graces can grow, the one indispensable condition of true fellowship with Jesus. That it should have been possible for men to say of those who claim to be seeking the higher holiness, that the profession has not been accompanied with increasing humility, is a loud call to all earnest Christians, however much or little truth there be in the charge, to prove that meekness and lowliness of heart are the chief mark by which they who follow the meek and lowly Lamb of God are to be known.

Humility: The Beauty of Holiness

Humility: The Glory of the Creature

'They shall cast their crowns before the throne, saying: Worthy art Thou, our Lord and our God, to receive the glory, and the honor and the power: for Thou didst create all things, and because of Thy will they were, and were created.' —REV. iv. 11.

WHEN God created the universe, it was with the one object of making the creature partaker of His perfection and blessedness, and so showing forth in it the glory of His love and wisdom and power. God wished to reveal Himself in and through created beings by communicating to them as much of His own goodness and glory as they were capable of receiving. But this communication was not a giving to the creature something which it could possess in itself, a certain life or goodness, of which it had the charge and disposal. By no means. But as God is the ever-living, ever-present, ever-acting One, who upholdeth all things by the word of His power, and in whom all things exist, the relation of the creature to God could only be one of unceasing, absolute, universal dependence. As truly as God by His power once created, so truly by that same power must God every moment maintain. The creature has not only to look back to the origin and first beginning of existence, and acknowledge that it there owes everything to God; its chief care, its highest virtue, its only happiness, now and through all eternity, is to present itself an empty vessel, in which God can dwell and manifest His power and goodness.

The life God bestows is imparted not once for all, but each moment continuously, by the unceasing operation of His mighty power. Humility, the place of entire dependence on God, is, from the very nature of things, the first duty and the highest virtue of the creature, and the root of every virtue.

And so pride, or the loss of this humility, is the root of every sin and evil. It was when the now fallen angels began to look upon themselves with self-complacency that they were led to disobedience, and were cast down from the light of heaven into outer darkness. Even so it was, when the serpent breathed the poison of his pride, the desire to be as God, into the hearts of our first parents, that they too fell from their high estate into all the wretchedness in which man is now sunk. In heaven and earth, pride, self-exaltation, is the gate and the birth, and the curse, of hell.[1]

---

[1] 'All this is to make it known the region of eternity that pride can degrade the highest angels into devils, and humility raise fallen flesh and blood to the thrones of angels. Thus, this is the great end of God raising a new creation out of a fallen kingdom of angels: for this end it stands in its state of war betwixt the fire and pride of fallen angels, and the humility of the Lamb of God, that the last trumpet may sound the great truth through the depths of eternity, that evil can have no beginning but from pride, and no end but from humility. The truth is this: Pride may die in you, or nothing of heaven can live in you. Under the banner of the truth, give yourself up to the meek and humble spirit of the holy Jesus. Humility must sow seed, or there can be no reaping in Heaven. Look not at pride only as an unbecoming temper, nor at humility only as a decent virtue: for the one is death, and the other is life; the one is all hell, the other is all heaven. So much as you have of pride within you, you have of the fallen angels alive in you; so much as you have of true humility, so much you have of the Lamb of God within you. Could you see what every stirring of pride does to your soul, you would beg of everything you meet to tear the viper from you, though with the loss of a hand or an eye. Could you see what a sweet, divine, transforming power there is in humility, how it expels the poison of your nature, and makes room for the Spirit of God to live in you, you would rather

Hence it follows that nothing can be our redemption, but the restoration of the lost humility, the original and only true relation of the creature to its God. And so Jesus came to bring humility back to earth, to make us partakers of it, and by it to save us. In heaven He humbled Himself to become man. The humility we see in Him possessed Him in heaven; it brought Him, He brought it, from there. Here on earth 'He humbled Himself, and became obedient unto death'; His humility gave His death its value, and so became our redemption. And now the salvation He imparts is nothing less and nothing else than a communication of His own life and death, His own disposition and spirit, His own humility, as the ground and root of His relation to God and His redeeming work. Jesus Christ took the place and fulfilled the destiny of man, as a creature, by His life of perfect humility. His humility is our salvation. His salvation is our humility.

And so the life of the saved ones, of the saints, must needs bear this stamp of deliverance from sin, and full restoration to their original state; their whole relation to God and man marked by an all-pervading humility. Without this there can be no true abiding in God's presence, or experience of His favor and the power of His Spirit; without this no abiding faith, or love or joy or strength. Humility is the only soil in which the graces root; the lack of humility is the sufficient explanation of every defect and failure. Humility is not so much a grace or virtue along with others; it is the root of all, because it alone takes the right attitude before God, and allows Him as God to do all.

God has so constituted us as reasonable beings, that the truer the insight into the real nature or the absolute need of a command, the readier and fuller will be our obedience to it. The call to humility has been too little regarded in the Church because its true nature and importance has been too little apprehended. It is not a something which we bring to God, or He bestows; it is simply *the sense of entire nothingness, which comes when we see how truly God is all, and in which we make way for God to be all.* When the creature realizes that this is the true nobility, and consents to be with his will, his mind, and his affections, the form, the vessel in which the life and glory of God are to work and manifest themselves, he sees that humility is simply acknowledging the truth of his position as creature, and yielding to God His place.

In the life of earnest Christians, of those who pursue and profess holiness, humility ought to be the chief mark of their uprightness. It is often said that it is not so. May not one reason be that in the teaching and example of the Church, it has never had that place of supreme importance which belongs to it? And that this, again, is owing to the neglect of this truth, that strong as sin is as a motive to humility, there is one of still wider and mightier influence, that which makes the angels, that which made Jesus, that which makes the holiest of saints in heaven, so humble; that the first and chief mark of the relation of the creature, the secret of his blessedness, is the humility and nothingness which leaves God free to be all?

I am sure there are many Christians who will confess that their experience has been very much like my own in this, that we had long known the Lord without realizing that meekness and lowliness of heart are to be the distinguishing feature of the disciple as they were of the Master. And further, that this humility is not a thing that will come of itself, but that it must be made the object of special desire and prayer and faith and practice. As we study the word, we shall see what very distinct and oft-repeated instructions Jesus gave His disciples on this point, and how slow they were in understanding Him. Let us, at the very commencement of our meditations, admit that there is nothing so natural to man, nothing so insidious and hidden from our sight, nothing so difficult and dangerous, as pride. Let us feel that nothing but a very determined and persevering waiting on God and Christ will discover how lacking we are in the grace of humility, and how impotent to obtain what we seek. Let us study the character of Christ until our souls are filled with the love and admiration of His lowliness. And let us believe that, when we are broken down under a sense of our pride, and our impotence to cast it out, Jesus Christ Himself will come in to impart this grace too, as a part of His wondrous life within us.

---

wish to be the footstool of all the world than want the smallest degree of it.' —Spirit of Prayer, Pt. II. p. 73, Edition of Moreton, Canterbury, 1893.

Humility: The Secret of Redemption

'Have this mind in you which was also in Christ Jesus: who emptied Himself; taking the form of a servant; and humbled Himself; becoming obedient even unto death. Wherefore God also highly exalted Him.' —PHIL. ii. 5-7.

NO tree can grow except on the root from which it sprang. Through all its existence it can only live with the life that was in the seed that gave it being. The full apprehension of this truth in its application to the first and the Second Adam cannot but help us greatly to understand both the need and the nature of the redemption there is in Jesus.

The Need. — When the Old Serpent, he who had been cast out from heaven for his pride, whose whole nature as devil was pride, spoke his words of temptation into the ear of Eve, these words carried with them the very poison of hell. And when she listened, and yielded her desire and her will to the prospect of being as God, knowing good and evil, the poison entered into her soul and blood and life, destroying forever that blessed humility and dependence upon God which would have been our everlasting happiness. And instead of this, her life and the life of the race that sprang from her became corrupted to its very root with that most terrible of all sins and all curses, the poison of Satan's own pride. All the wretchedness of which this world has been the scene, all its wars and bloodshed among the nations, all its selfishness and suffering, all its ambitions and jealousies, all its broken hearts and embittered lives, with all its daily unhappiness, have their origin in what this cursed, hellish pride, either our own, or that of others, has brought us. It is pride that made redemption needful; it is from our pride we need above everything to be redeemed. And our insight into the need of redemption will largely depend upon our knowledge of the terrible nature of the power that has entered our being.

No tree can grow except on the root from which it sprang. The power that Satan brought from hell, and cast into man's life, is working daily, hourly, with mighty power throughout the world. Men suffer from it; they fear and fight and flee it; and yet they know not whence it comes, whence it has its terrible supremacy. No wonder they do not know where or how it is to be overcome. Pride has its root and strength in a terrible spiritual power, outside of us as well as within us; as needful as it is that we confess and deplore it as our very own, is to know it in its Satanic origin. If this leads us to utter despair of ever conquering or casting it out, it will lead us all the sooner to that supernatural power in which alone our deliverance is to be found—the redemption of the Lamb of God. The hopeless struggle against the workings of self and pride within us may indeed become still more hopeless as we think of the power of darkness behind it all; the utter despair will fit us the better for realizing and accepting a power and a life outside of ourselves too, even the humility of heaven as brought down and brought nigh by the Lamb of God, to cast out Satan and his pride.

No tree can grow except on the root from which it sprang. Even as we need to look to the first Adam and his fall to know the power of the sin within us, we need to know well the Second Adam and His power to give within us a life of humility as real and abiding and overmastering as has been that of pride. We have our life from and in Christ, as truly, yea more truly, than from and in Adam. We are to walk 'rooted in Him,' 'holding fast the Head from whom the whole body increaseth with the increase of God.' The life of God which in the incarnation entered human nature, is the root in which we are to stand and grow; it is the same almighty power that worked there, and thence onward to the resurrection, which works daily in us. Our one need is to study and know and trust the life that has been revealed in Christ as the life that is now ours, and waits for our consent to gain possession and mastery of our whole being.

In this view it is of inconceivable importance that we should have right thoughts of what Christ is, of what really constitutes Him the Christ, and specially of what may be counted His chief characteristic, the root and essence of all His character as our Redeemer. There can be but one answer: it is His humility. What is the incarnation but His heavenly humility, His emptying Himself and becoming man? What is His life on earth but humility; His taking the form of a servant? And what is His atonement but humility? 'He humbled Himself and became obedient unto death.' And what is His ascension and His glory, but humility exalted to the throne and crowned with glory? 'He humbled Himself, therefore God highly exalted Him.' In heaven, where He was with the Father, in His birth, in His life, in His death, in His sitting on the throne, it is all, it is nothing but humility. Christ is the humility of God embodied in human nature; the Eternal Love humbling itself, clothing itself in the garb of meekness and gentleness, to win and serve and save us. As the love and condescension of God makes Him the benefactor and helper and servant of all, so Jesus of necessity was the Incarnate Humility. And so He is still in the midst of the throne, the meek and lowly Lamb of God.

If this be the root of the tree, its nature must be seen in every branch and leaf and fruit. If humility be the first, the all-including grace of the life of Jesus, —if humility be the secret of His atonement, —then the health and strength of our spiritual life will entirely depend upon our putting this grace first too, and making humility the chief thing we admire in Him, the chief thing we ask of Him, the one thing for which we sacrifice all else.[2]

Is it any wonder that the Christian life is so often feeble and fruitless, when the very root of the Christ life is neglected, is unknown? Is it any wonder that the joy of salvation is so little felt, when that in which Christ found it and brings it, is so little sought? Until a humility which will rest in nothing less than the end and death of self; which gives up all the honor of men as Jesus did, to seek the honor that comes from God alone; which absolutely makes and counts itself nothing, that God may be all, that the Lord alone may be exalted, —until such a humility be what we seek in Christ above our chief joy, and welcome at any price, there is very little hope of a religion that will conquer the world.

I cannot too earnestly plead with my reader, if possibly his attention has never yet been specially directed to the want there is of humility within him or around him, to pause and ask whether he sees much of the spirit of the meek and lowly Lamb of God in those who are called by His name. Let him consider how all want of love, all indifference to the needs, the feelings, the weakness of others; all sharp and hasty judgments and utterances, so often excused under the plea of being outright and honest; all manifestations of temper and touchiness and irritation; all feelings of bitterness and estrangement, have their root in nothing but pride, that ever seeks itself, and his eyes will be opened to see how a dark, shall I not say a devilish pride, creeps in almost everywhere, the assemblies of the saints not excepted. Let him begin to ask what would be the effect, if in himself and around him, if towards fellow-saints and the world, believers were really permanently guided by the humility of Jesus; and let him say if the cry of our whole heart, night and day, ought not to be, Oh for the humility of Jesus in myself and all around me! Let him honestly fix his heart on his own lack of the humility which has been revealed in the likeness of Christ's life, and in the whole character of His redemption, and he will begin to feel as if he had never yet really known what Christ and His salvation is.

Believer! *study the humility of Jesus*. This is the secret, the hidden root of thy redemption. Sink down into it deeper day by day. Believe with thy whole heart that this Christ, whom God has given thee, even as His divine humility wrought the work for thee, will enter in to dwell and work within thee too, and make thee what the Father would have thee be.

---

2 'We need to know two things: 1. That our salvation consists wholly in being saved from ourselves, or that which we are by nature; 2. That in the whole nature of things nothing could be this salvation or savior to us but such a humility of God as is beyond all expression. Hence the first unalterable term of the Savior to fallen man: Except a man denies himself, he cannot be My disciple. Self is the whole evil of fallen nature; self-denial is our capacity of being saved; humility is our savior.... Self is the root, the branches, the tree, of all the evil of our fallen state. All the evils of fallen angels and men have their birth in the pride of self. On the other hand, all the virtues of the heavenly life are the virtues of humility. It is humility alone that makes the unpassable gulf between heaven and hell. What is then, or in what lies, the great struggle for eternal life? It all lies in the strife between pride and humility: pride and humility are the two master powers, the two kingdoms in strife for the eternal possession of man. There never was, nor ever will be, but one humility, and that is the one humility of Christ. Pride and self have the all of man, till man has his all from Christ. He therefore only fights the good fight whose strife is that the self-idolatrous nature which he hath from Adam may be brought to death by the supernatural humility of Christ brought to life in him.' —W. Law, Address to the Clergy, p. 52.

Humility in the Life of Jesus

'I am in the midst of you as he that serveth.' —LUKE xxii. 26.

IN the Gospel of John we have the inner life of our Lord laid open to us. Jesus speaks frequently of His relation to the Father, of the motives by which He is guided, of His consciousness of the power and spirit in which He acts. Though the word humble does not occur, we shall nowhere in Scripture see so clearly wherein His humility consisted. We have already said that this grace is in truth nothing but that simple consent of the creature to let God be all, in virtue of which it surrenders itself to His working alone. In Jesus we shall see how both as the Son of God in heaven, and as man upon earth, He took the place of entire subordination, and gave God the honor and the glory which is due to Him. And what He taught so often was made true to Himself: 'He that humbleth him: shall be exalted.' As it is written, 'He humbled Himself, therefore God highly exalted Him.'

Listen to the words in which our Lord speaks of His relation to the Father, and how unceasingly He uses the words *not*, and *nothing*, of Himself. The *not I*, in which Paul expresses his relation to Christ, is the very spirit of what Christ says of His relation the Father.

'The Son can do *nothing* of Himself' (John v. 19).

'I can of My own self do *nothing*; My judgment is just, because I seek *not* Mine own will' (John v 30).

'I receive *not* glory from men' (John v. 41).

'I am come *not* to do Mine own will' (John vi. 38).

'My teaching is *not* Mine' (John vii. 16).

'I am *not* come of Myself' (John vii. 28).

'I do *nothing* of Myself' (John vii. 28).

'I have *not* come of Myself, but He sent Me' (John viii. 42).

'I seek *not* Mine own glory' (John viii. 50).

'The words that I say, I speak *not* from Myself' (John xiv. 10).

'The word which ye hear is *not* Mine' (John xiv. 24).

These words open to us the deepest roots of Christ's life and work. They tell us how it was that the Almighty God was able to work His mighty redemptive work through Him. They show what Christ counted the state of heart which became Him as the Son of the Father. They teach us what the essential nature and life is of that redemption which Christ accomplished and now communicates. It is this: He was nothing, that God might be all. He resigned Himself with His will and His powers entirely for the Father to work in Him. Of His own power, His own will, and His own glory, of His whole mission with all His works and His teaching,—of all this He said, It is not I; I am nothing; I have given Myself to the Father to work; I am nothing, the Father is all.

This life of entire self-abnegation, of absolute submission and dependence upon the Father's will, Christ found to be one of perfect peace and joy. He lost nothing by giving all to God. God honored His trust, and did all for Him, and then exalted Him to His own right hand in glory. And because Christ had thus humbled Himself before God, and God was ever before Him, He found it possible to humble Himself before men too, and to be the Servant of all. His humility was simply the surrender of Himself to God, to allow Him to do in Him what He pleased, whatever men around might say of Him, or do to Him.

It is in this state of mind, in this spirit and disposition, that the redemption of Christ has its virtue and efficacy. It is to bring us to this disposition that we are made partakers of Christ. This is the true self-denial to which our Savior calls us, the acknowledgment that self has nothing good in it, except as an empty vessel which God must fill, and that its claim to be or do anything may not for a moment be allowed. It is in this, above and before everything, in which the conformity to Jesus consists, the being and doing nothing of ourselves, that God may be all.

Here we have the root and nature of true humility. It is because this is not understood or sought after, that our humility is so superficial and so feeble. We must learn of Jesus, how He is meek and lowly of heart. He teaches us where true humility takes its rise and finds its strength—in the knowledge that it is God who worketh all in all, that our place is to yield to Him in perfect resignation and dependence, in full consent to be and to do nothing of ourselves. This is the life Christ came to reveal and to impart—a life to God that came through death to sin and self. If we feel that this life is too high for us and beyond our reach, it must but the more urge us to seek it in Him; it is the indwelling Christ who will live in us this life, meek and lowly. If we long for this, let us, meantime, above everything, seek the holy secret of the knowledge of the nature of God, as He every moment works all in all; the secret, of which all nature and every creature, and above all, every child of God, is to be the witness, —that it is nothing but a vessel, a channel, through which the living God can manifest the riches of His wisdom, power, and goodness. The root of all virtue and grace, of all faith and acceptable worship, is that we know that we have nothing but what we receive, and bow in deepest humility to wait upon God for it.

It was because this humility was not only a temporary sentiment, wakened up and brought into exercise when He thought of God, but the very spirit of His whole life, that Jesus was just as humble in His intercourse with men as with God. He felt Himself the Servant of God for the men whom God made and loved; as a natural consequence, He counted Himself the Servant of men, that through Him God might do His work of love. He never for a moment thought of seeking His honor, or asserting His power to vindicate Himself. His whole spirit was that of a life yielded to God to work in. It is not until Christians study the humility of Jesus as the very essence of His redemption, as the very blessedness of the life of the Son of God, as the only true relation to the Father, and therefore as that which Jesus must give us if we are to have any part with Him, that the terrible lack of actual, heavenly, manifest humility will become a burden and a sorrow, and our ordinary religion be set aside to secure this, the first and the chief of the marks of the Christ within us.

Brother, are you clothed with humility? Ask your daily life. Ask Jesus. Ask your friends. Ask the world. And begin to praise God that there is opened up to you in Jesus a heavenly humility of which you have hardly known, and through which a heavenly blessedness you possibly have never yet tasted can come in to you.

Humility in the Teaching of Jesus

'Learn of Me, for I am meek and lowly of heart.' —MATT. xi. 29. 'Whosoever will be chief among you, let him be your servant, even as the Son of Man came to serve.' —MATT. xx. 27.

WE have seen humility in the life of Christ, as He laid open His heart to us: let us listen to His teaching. There we shall hear how He speaks of it, and how far He expects men, and specially His disciples, to be humble as He was. Let us carefully study the passages, which I can scarce do more than quote, to receive the full impression of how often and how earnestly He taught it: it may help us to realize what He asks of us.

1. Look at the commencement of His ministry. In the Beatitudes with which the Sermon on the Mount opens, He speaks: *'Blessed are the poor in spirit; for theirs is the kingdom of heaven. Blessed are the meek; for they shall inherit the earth.'* The very first words of His proclamation of the kingdom of heaven reveal the open gate through which alone we enter. The poor, who have nothing in themselves, to them the kingdom comes. The meek, who seek nothing in themselves, theirs the earth shall be. The blessings of heaven and earth are for the lowly. For the heavenly and the earthly life, humility is the secret of blessing.

2. *'Learn of Me; for I am meek and lowly of heart, and ye shall find rest for your souls.'* Jesus offers Himself as Teacher. He tells what the spirit both is, which we shall find Him as Teacher, and which we can learn and receive from Him. Meekness and lowliness the one thing He offers us; in it we shall find perfect rest of soul. Humility is to be a salvation.

3. The disciples had been disputing who would be the greatest in the kingdom, and had agreed to ask the Master (Luke 9:46; Matt. 18:3). He set a child in their midst and said, *'Whosoever shall humble himself as this little child, shall be exalted.'* 'Who the greatest in the kingdom of heaven?' The question is indeed a far-reaching one. What will be the chief distinction in the heavenly kingdom? The answer, none but Jesus would have given. The chief glory of heaven, the true heavenly-mindedness, the chief of the graces, is humility. *'He that is least among you, the same shall be great.'*

4. The sons of Zebedee had asked Jesus to sit on His right and left, the highest place in the kingdom. Jesus said it was not His to give, but the Father's, who would give it to those for whom it was prepared. They must not look or ask for it. Their thought must be of the cup and the baptism of

humiliation. And then He added, *'Whosoever will be chief among you, let him be your servant. Even as the Son of Man came to serve.'* Humility, as it is the mark of Christ the heavenly, will be the one standard of glory in heaven: the lowliest is the nearest to God. The primacy in the Church is promised to the humblest.

5. Speaking to the multitude and the disciples, of the Pharisees and their love of the chief seats, Christ said once again (Matt. xxxiii. 11), *'He that is greatest among you shall be your servant.'* Humiliation is the only ladder to honor in God's kingdom.

6. On another occasion, in the house of a Pharisee, He spoke the parable of the guest who would be invited to come up higher (Luke xiv. 1-11), and added, *'For whosoever exalteth himself shall be abased; and he that humbleth himself shall be exalted.'* The demand is inexorable; there is no other way. Self-abasement alone will be exalted.

7. After the parable of the Pharisee and the Publican, Christ spake again (Luke xviii. 14), *'Everyone that exalteth himself shall be abased; and he that humbleth himself shall be exalted.'* In the temple and presence and worship of God, everything is worthless that is not pervaded by deep, true humility towards God and men.

8. After washing the disciples' feet, Jesus said (John xiii. 14), *'If I then, the Lord and Master, have washed your feet, ye also ought to wash one another's feet.'* The authority of command, and example, every thought, either of obedience or conformity, make humility the first and most essential element of discipleship.

9. At the Holy Supper table, the disciples still disputed who should be greatest (Luke xxii. 26). Jesus said, *'He that is greatest among you, let him be as the younger; and he that is chief, as he that doth serve. I am among you as he that serveth.'* The path in which Jesus walked, and which He opened up for us, the power and spirit in which He wrought out salvation, and to which He saves us, is ever the humility that makes me the servant of all.

How little this is preached. How little it is practiced. How little the lack of it is felt or confessed. I do not say, how few attain to it, some recognizable measure of likeness to Jesus in His humility. But how few ever think, of making it a distinct object of continual desire or prayer. How little the world has seen it. How little has it been seen even in the inner circle of the Church.

'Whosoever will be chief among you, let him be your servant.' Would God that it might be given us to believe that Jesus means this! We all know what the character of a faithful servant or slave implies. Devotion to the master's interests, thoughtful study and care to please him, delight in his prosperity and honor and happiness. There are servants on earth in whom these dispositions have been seen, and to whom the name of servant has never been anything but a glory. To how many of us has it not been a new joy in the Christian life to know that we may yield ourselves as servants, as slaves to God, and to find that His service is our highest liberty, —the liberty from sin and self? We need now to learn another lesson, —that Jesus calls us to be servants of one another, and that, as we accept it heartily, this service too will be a most blessed one, a new and fuller liberty too from sin and self. At first it may appear hard; this is only because of the pride which still counts itself something. If once we learn that to be nothing before God is the glory of the creature, the spirit of Jesus, the joy of heaven, we shall welcome with our whole heart the discipline we may have in serving even those who try to vex us. When our own heart is set upon this, the true sanctification, we shall study each word of Jesus on self-abasement with new zest, and no place will be too low, and no stooping too deep, and no service too mean or too long continued, if we may but share and prove the fellowship with Him who spake, 'I am among you as he that serveth.'

Brethren, here is the path to the higher life. Down, lower down! This was what Jesus ever said to the disciples who were thinking of being great in the kingdom, and of sitting on His right hand and His left. Seek not, ask not for exaltation; that is God's work. Look to it that you abase and humble yourselves, and take no place before God or man but that of servant; that is your work; let that be your one purpose and prayer. God is faithful. Just as water ever seeks and fills the lowest place, so the moment God finds the creature abased and empty, His glory and power flow in to exalt and to bless. He that humbleth himself—that must be our one care—shall be exalted; that is God's care; by His mighty power and in His great love He will do it.

Men sometimes speak as if humility and meekness would rob us of what is noble and bold and manlike. Oh that all would believe that this is the nobility of the kingdom of heaven, that this is the royal spirit that the King of heaven displayed, that this is Godlike, to humble oneself, to become the servant of all! This is the path to the gladness and the glory of Christ's presence ever in us, His power ever resting on us.

Jesus, the meek and lowly One, calls us to learn of Him the path to God. Let us study the words we have been reading, until our heart is filled with the thought: My one need is humility. And let us believe that what He shows, He gives; what He is, He imparts. As the meek and lowly One, He will come in and dwell in the longing heart.

Humility in the Disciples of Jesus

'Let him that is chief among you be as he that doth serve.' —*LUKE xxii. 26*

WE have studied humility in the person and teaching of Jesus; let us now look for it in the circle of His chosen companions—the twelve apostles. If, in the lack of it we find in them, the contrast between Christ and men is brought out more clearly, it will help us to appreciate the mighty change which Pentecost wrought in them, and prove how real our participation can be in the perfect triumph of Christ's humility over the pride Satan had breathed into man.

In the texts quoted from the teaching of Jesus, we have already seen what the occasions were on which the disciples had proved how entirely wanting they were in the grace of humility. Once, they had been disputing the way which of them should be the greatest Another time, the sons of Zebedee with their mother had asked for the first places—the seat on the right hand and the left. And, later on, at the Supper table on the last night, there was again a contention which should be accounted the greatest. Not that there were not moments when they indeed humbled themselves before their Lord. So it was with Peter when he cried out, 'Depart from me, Lord, for I am a sinful man.' So, too, with the disciples when they fell down and worshipped Him who had stilled the storm. But such occasional expressions of humility only bring out into stronger relief what was the habitual tone of their mind, as shown in the natural and spontaneous revelation given at other times of the place and the power of self. The study of the meaning of all this will teach us most important lessons.

First, *How much there may be of earnest and active, religion while humility is still sadly wanting.* —See it in the disciples. There was in them fervent attachment to Jesus. They had forsaken all for Him. The Father had revealed to them that He was the Christ of God. They believed in Him, they loved Him, they obeyed His commandments. They had forsaken all to follow Him. When others went back, they clave to Him. They were ready to die with Him. But deeper down than all this there was a dark power, of the existence and the hideousness of which they were hardly conscious, which had to be slain and cast out, ere they could be the witnesses of the power of Jesus to save. It is even so still. We may find professors and ministers, evangelists and workers, missionaries and teachers, in whom the gifts of the Spirit are many and manifest, and who are the channels of blessing to multitudes, but of whom, when the testing time comes, or closer intercourse gives fuller knowledge, it is only too painfully manifest that the grace of humility, as an abiding characteristic, is scarce to be seen. All tends to confirm the lesson that humility is one of the chief and the highest graces; one of the most difficult of attainment; one to which our first and chiefest efforts ought to be directed; one that only comes in power, when the fullness of the Spirit makes us partakers of the indwelling Christ, and He lives within us.

Second, *How impotent all external teaching and all personal effort is, to conquer pride or give the meek and lowly heart.* —For three years the disciples had been in the training school of Jesus. He had told them what the chief lesson was He wished to teach them: 'Learn of Me, for I am meek and lowly in heart.' Time after time He had spoken to them, to the Pharisees, to the multitude, of humility as the only path to the glory of God. He had not only lived before them as the Lamb of God in His divine humility, He had more than once unfolded to them the inmost secret of His life: 'The Son of Man came not to be served, but to serve'; 'I am among you as one that serveth.' He had washed their feet, and told them they were to follow His example. And yet all had availed but little. At the Holy Supper there was still the contention as to who should be greatest. They had doubtless often tried to learn His lessons, and firmly resolved not again to grieve Him. But all in vain. To teach them and us the much needed lesson, that no outward instruction, not even of Christ Himself; no argument however convincing; no sense of the beauty of humility, however deep; no personal resolve or effort, however sincere and earnest, —can cast out the devil of pride. When Satan casts out Satan, it is only to enter afresh in a mightier, though more hidden power. Nothing can avail but this, that the new nature in its divine humility be revealed in power to take the place of the old, to become as truly our very nature as that ever was.

Third, *It is only by the indwelling of Christ in His divine humility that we become truly humble.* —We have our pride from another, from Adam; we must have our humility from Another too. Pride is ours, and rules in us with such terrible power, because it is ourself, our very nature. Humility must be ours in the same way; it must be our very self, our very nature. As natural and easy as it has been to be proud, it must be, it will be, to be humble. The promise is, 'Where,' even in the heart, 'sin abounded, grace did abound more exceedingly.' All Christ's teaching of His disciples, and all their vain efforts, were the needful preparation for His entering into them in divine power, to give and be in them what He had taught them to desire. In His death He destroyed the power of the devil, He put away sin, and effected an everlasting redemption. In His resurrection He received from the Father an entirely new life, the life of man in the power of God, capable of being communicated to men, and entering and renewing and filling their lives with His divine power. In His ascension He received the Spirit of the Father, through whom He might do what He could not do while upon earth, make Himself one with those He loved, actually live their life for them, so that they could live before the Father in a humility like His, because it was Himself who lived and breathed in them. And on Pentecost He came and took possession. The work of preparation and conviction, the awakening of desire and hope which His teaching had effected, was perfected by the mighty change that Pentecost wrought. And the lives and the epistles of James and Peter and John bear witness that all was changed, and that the spirit of the meek and suffering Jesus had indeed possession of them.

What shall we say to these things? Among my readers I am sure there is more than one class. There may be some who have never yet thought very specially of the matter, and cannot at once realize its immense importance as a life question for the Church and its every member. There are others who have felt condemned for their shortcomings, and have put forth very earnest efforts, only to fail and be discouraged. Others, again, may be able to give joyful testimony of spiritual blessing and power, and yet there has never been the needed conviction of what those around them still see as wanting. And still others may be able to witness that in regard to this grace too the Lord has given deliverance and victory, while He has taught them how much they still need and may expect out of the fullness of Jesus. To whichever class we belong, may I urge the pressing need there is for our all seeking a still deeper conviction of the unique place that humility holds in the religion of Christ, and the utter impossibility of the Church or the believer being what Christ would have them be, as long as *His humility is not recognized as His chief glory, His first command, and our highest blessedness.* Let us consider deeply how far the disciples were advanced while this grace was still so terribly lacking, and let us pray to God that other gifts may not so satisfy us, that we never grasp the fact that the absence of this grace is the secret cause why the power of God cannot do its mighty work. It is only where we, like the Son, truly know and show that we can do nothing of ourselves, that God will do all.

It is when the truth of an indwelling Christ takes the place it claims in the experience of believers, that the Church will put on her beautiful garments and humility be seen in her teachers and members as the beauty of holiness.

Humility in Daily Life

'He that loveth not his brother whom he hath seen, how can he love God whom he hath not seen?' —1 JOHN iv. 20.

WHAT a solemn thought, that our love to God will be measured by our everyday intercourse with men and the love it displays; and that our love to God will be found to be a delusion, except was its truth is proved in standing the test of daily life with our fellowmen. It is even so with our humility. It is easy to think we humble ourselves before God: humility towards men will be the only sufficient proof that our humility before God is real; that humility has taken up its abode in us; and become our very nature; that we actually, like Christ, have made ourselves of no reputation. When in the presence of God lowliness of heart has become, not a posture we pray to Him, but the very spirit of our life, it will manifest itself in all our bearing towards our brethren. The lesson is one of deep import: the only humility that is really ours is not that which we try to show before God in prayer, but that which we carry with us, and carry out, in our ordinary conduct; the insignificances of daily life are the importances and the tests of eternity, because they prove what really is the spirit that possesses us. It is in our most unguarded moments that we really show and see what we are. To know the humble man, to know how the humble man behaves, you must follow him in the common course of daily life.

Is not this what Jesus taught? It was when the disciples disputed who should be greatest; when He saw how the Pharisees loved the chief place at feasts and the chief seats in the synagogues; when He had given them the example of washing their feet, —that He taught His lessons of humility. Humility before God is nothing if not proved in humility before men.

It is even so in the teaching of Paul. To the Romans He writes: 'In honor preferring one *another*'; 'Set not your mind on high things, but condescend to *those that are lowly*.' 'Be not wise in your own conceit.' To the Corinthians: 'Love,' and there is no love without humility as its root, 'vaunteth not itself, is not puffed up, seeketh not its own, is not provoked.' To the Galatians: 'Through love be servants *one of another*. Let us not be desirous of vainglory, provoking *one another*, envying *one another.*' To the Ephesians, immediately after the three wonderful chapters on the heavenly life: 'Therefore, walk with all lowliness and meekness, with long-suffering, forbearing *one another* in love'; 'Giving thanks always, subjecting yourselves *one to another* in the fear of Christ.' To the Philippians: 'Doing nothing through faction or vainglory, but in lowliness of mind, each counting *other* better than himself. Have the mind in you which was also in Christ Jesus, who emptied Himself, taking the form of a servant, and humbled Himself.' And to the Colossians: 'Put on a heart of compassion, kindness, humility, meekness, long-suffering, forbearing *one another*, and forgiving *each other*, even as the Lord forgave you.' It is in our relation to one another, in our treatment of one another, that the true lowliness of mind and the heart of humility are to be seen. Our humility before God has no value, but as it prepares us to reveal the humility of Jesus to our fellow-men. Let us study humility in daily life in the light of these words.

The humble man seeks at all times to act up to the rule, *'In honor preferring one another; Servants one of another; Each counting others better than himself; Subjecting yourselves one to another.'* The question is often asked, how we can count others better than ourselves, when we see that they are far below us in wisdom and in holiness, in natural gifts, or in grace received. The question proves at once how little we understand what real lowliness of mind is. True humility comes when, in the light of God, we have seen ourselves to be nothing, have consented to part with and cast away self, to let God be all. The soul that has done this, and can say, So have I lost myself in finding Thee, no longer compares itself with others. It has given up forever every thought of self in God's presence; it meets its fellow-men as one who is nothing, and seeks nothing for itself; who is a servant of God, and for His sake a servant of all. A faithful servant may be wiser than the master, and yet retain the true spirit and posture of the servant. The humble man looks upon every, the feeblest and unworthiest, child of God, and honors him and prefers him in honor as the son of a King. The spirit of Him who washed the disciples' feet, makes it a joy to us to be indeed the least, to be servants one of another.

The humble man feels no jealousy or envy. He can praise God when others are preferred and blessed before him. He can bear to hear others praised and himself forgotten, because in God's presence he has learnt to say with Paul, 'I am nothing.' He has received the spirit of Jesus, who pleased not Himself, and sought not His own honor, as the spirit of his life.

Amid what are considered the temptations to impatience and touchiness, to hard thoughts and sharp words, which come from the failings and sins of fellow-Christians, the humble man carries the oft-repeated injunction in his heart, and shows it in his life, *'Forbearing one another, and forgiving one another, even as the Lord forgave you.'* He has learnt that in putting on the Lord Jesus he *has put on the heart of compassion, kindness, humility, meekness, and long-suffering.* Jesus has taken the place of self, and it is not an impossibility to forgive as Jesus forgave. His humility does not consist merely in thoughts or words of self-depreciation, but, as Paul puts it, in 'a heart of humility,' encompassed by compassion and kindness, meekness and long-suffering, —the sweet and lowly gentleness recognized as the mark of the Lamb of God.

In striving after the higher experiences of the Christian life, the believer is often in danger of aiming at and rejoicing in what one might call the more human, the manly, virtues, such as boldness, joy, contempt of the world, zeal, self-sacrifice, —even the old Stoics taught and practiced these, —while the deeper and gentler, the diviner and more heavenly graces, those which Jesus first taught upon earth, because He brought them from heaven; those which are more distinctly connected with

His cross and the death of self, —poverty of spirit, meekness, humility, lowliness, —are scarcely thought of or valued. Therefore, let us put on a heart of compassion, kindness, humility, meekness, long-suffering; and let us prove our Christlikeness, not only in our zeal for saving the lost, but before all in our intercourse with the brethren, forbearing and forgiving one another, *even as the Lord forgave us.*

Fellow-Christians, do let us study the Bible portrait of the humble man. And let us ask our brethren, and ask the world, whether they recognize in us the likeness to the original. Let us be content with nothing less than taking each of these texts as the promise of what God will work in us, as the revelation in words of what the Spirit of Jesus will give as a birth within us. And let each failure and shortcoming simply urge us to turn humbly and meekly to the meek and lowly Lamb of God, in the assurance that where He is enthroned in the heart, His humility and gentleness will be one of the streams of living water that flow from within us.[3]

Once again I repeat what I have said before. I feel deeply that we have very little conception of what the Church suffers from the lack of this divine humility, —the nothingness that makes room for God to prove His power. It is not long since a Christian, of an humble, loving spirit, acquainted with not a few mission stations of various societies, expressed his deep sorrow that in some cases the spirit of love and forbearance was sadly lacking. Men and women, who in Europe could each choose their own circle of friends, brought close together with others of uncongenial minds, find it hard to bear, and to love, and to keep the unity of the Spirit in the bond of peace. And those who should have been fellow-helpers of each other's joy, became a hindrance and a weariness. And all for the one reason, the lack of the humility which counts itself nothing, which rejoices in becoming and being counted the least, and only seeks, like Jesus, to be the servant, the helper and comforter of others, even the lowest and unworthiest.

And whence comes it that men who have joyfully given up themselves for Christ, find it so hard to give up themselves for their brethren? Is not the blame with the Church? It has so little taught its sons that the humility of Christ is the first of the virtues, the best of all the graces and powers of the Spirit. It has so little proved that a Christlike humility is what it, like Christ, places and preaches first, as what is in very deed needed, and possible too. But let us not be discouraged. Let the discovery of the lack of this grace stir us to larger expectation from God. Let us look upon every brother who tries or vexes us, as God's means of grace, God's instrument for our purification, for our exercise of the humility Jesus our Life breathes within us. And let us have such faith in the All of God, and the nothing of self, that, as nothing in our own eyes, we may, in God's power, only seek to serve one another in love.

Humility and Holiness

'Which say, Stand by thyself; for I am holier than thou.' —ISAIAH lxv. 5.

WE speak of the Holiness movement in our times, and praise God for it. We hear a great deal of seekers after holiness and professors of holiness, of holiness teaching and holiness meetings. The blessed truths of holiness in Christ, and holiness by faith, are being emphasized as never before. The great test of whether the holiness we profess to seek or to attain, is truth and life, will be *whether it be manifest in the increasing humility it produces.* In the creature, humility is the one thing needed to allow God's holiness to dwell in him and shine through him. In Jesus, the Holy One of God who makes us holy, a divine humility was the secret of His life and His death and His exaltation; the one infallible test of our holiness will be the humility before God and men which marks us. Humility is the bloom and the beauty of holiness.

The chief mark of counterfeit holiness is its lack of humility. Every seeker after holiness needs to be on his guard, lest unconsciously what was begun in the spirit be perfected in the flesh, and pride creep in where its presence is least expected. Two men went up into the temple to pray: the one a Pharisee, the other a publican. There is no place or position so sacred but the Pharisee can enter there. Pride can lift its head in the very temple of God, and make His worship the scene of its

[3] 'I knew Jesus, and He was very precious to my soul: but I found something in me that would not keep sweet and patient and kind. I did what I could to keep it down, but it was there. I besought Jesus to do something for me, and when I gave Him my will, He came to my heart, and took out all that would not be sweet, all that would not be kind, all that would not be patient, and then He shut the door.' —George Foxe

self exaltation. Since the time Christ so exposed his pride, the Pharisee has put on the garb of the publican, and the confessor of deep sinfulness equally with the professor of the highest holiness, must be on the watch. Just when We are most anxious to have our heart the temple of God, we shall find the two men coming up to pray. And the publican will find that his danger is not from the Pharisee beside him, who despises him, but the Pharisee within who commends and exalts. In God's temple, when we think we are in the holiest of all, in the presence of His holiness, let us beware of pride. 'Now there was a day when the sons of God came to present themselves before the Lord, and Satan came also among them.'

'God, I thank thee, I am not as the rest of men, or even as this publican.' It is in that which is just cause for thanksgiving, it is in the very thanksgiving which we render to God, it may be in the very confession that God has done it all, that self finds its cause of complacency. Yes, even when in the temple the language of penitence and trust in God's mercy alone is heard, the Pharisee may take up the note of praise, and in thanking God be congratulating himself. Pride can clothe itself in the garments of praise or of penitence. Even though the words, 'I am not as the rest of men' are rejected and condemned, their spirit may too often be found in our feelings and language towards our fellow-worshippers and fellow-men. Would you know if this really is so, just listen to the way in which Churches and Christians often speak of one another. How little of the meekness and gentleness of Jesus is to be seen. It is so little remembered that deep humility must be the keynote of what the servants of Jesus say of themselves or each other. Is there not many a Church or assembly of the saints, many a mission or convention, many a society or committee, even many a mission away in heathendom, where the harmony has been disturbed and the work of God hindered, because men who are counted saints have proved in touchiness and haste and impatience, in self-defense and self-assertion, in sharp judgments and unkind words, that they did not each reckon others better than themselves, and that their holiness has but little in it of the meekness of the saints?[4] In their spiritual history men may have had times of great humbling and brokenness, but what a different thing this is from being clothed with humility, from having an humble spirit, from having that lowliness of mind in which each counts himself the servant of others, and so shows forth the very mind which was also in Jesus Christ.

'Stand by; for I am holier than thou!' What a parody on holiness! Jesus the Holy One is the humble One: the holiest will ever be the humblest. There is none holy but God: we have as much of holiness as we have of God. And according to what we have of God will be our real humility, because humility is nothing but the disappearance of self in the vision that God is all. The holiest will be the humblest. Alas! though the barefaced boasting Jew of the days of Isaiah is not often to be found, —even our manners have taught us not to speak thus, how often his spirit is still seen, whether in the treatment of fellow-saints or of the children of the world. In the spirit in which opinions are given, and work is undertaken, and faults are exposed, how often, though the garb be that of the publican, the voice is still that of the Pharisee: 'Oh God, I thank Thee that I am not as other men.'

And is there, then, such humility to be found, that men shall indeed still count themselves 'less than the least of all saints,' the servants of all? There is. 'Love vaunteth not itself, is not puffed up, seeketh not its own.' Where the spirit of love is shed abroad in the heart, where the divine nature comes to a full birth where Christ the meek and lowly Lamb of God is truly formed within, there is given the power of a perfect love that forgets itself and finds its blessedness in blessing others, in bearing with them and honoring them, however feeble they be. Where this love enters, there God enters. And where God has entered in His power, and reveals Himself as All, there the creature becomes nothing. And where the creature becomes nothing before God; it cannot be anything but humble towards the fellow-creature. The presence of God becomes not a thing of times and seasons, but the covering under which the soul ever dwells, and its deep abasement before God becomes the holy place of His presence whence all its words and works proceed.

---

[4] ME is a most exacting personage, requiring the best seat and the highest place for itself, and feeling grievously wounded if its claim is not recognized. Most of the quarrels among Christian workers arise from the clamoring of this gigantic ME. How few of us understand the true secret of taking our seats in the lowest rooms. —Mrs. Smith, Everyday Religion.

May God teach us that our thoughts and words and feelings concerning our fellowmen are His test of our humility towards Him, and that our humility before Him is the only power that can enable us to be always humble with our fellow-men. Our humility must be the life of Christ, the Lamb of God, within us.

Let all teachers of holiness, whether in the pulpit or on the platform, and all seekers after holiness, whether in the closet or the convention, take warning. There is no pride so dangerous, because none so subtle and insidious, as the pride of holiness. It is not that a man ever says, or even thinks, 'Stand by; I am holier than thou.' No, indeed, the thought would be regarded with abhorrence. But there grows up, all unconsciously, a hidden habit of soul, which feels complacency its attainments, and cannot help seeing how far it is in advance of others. It can be recognized, not always in any special self-assertion or self-laudation, but simply in the absence of that deep self-abasement which cannot but be the mark of the soul that has seen the glory of God (Job xlii. 5, 6; Isa. vi. 5). It reveals itself, not only in words or thoughts, but in a tone, a way of speaking of others, in which those who have the gift of spiritual discernment cannot but recognize the power of self. Even the world with its keen eyes notices it, and points to it as a proof that the profession of a heavenly life does not bear any specially heavenly fruits. O brethren! let us beware. Unless we make, with each advance in what we think holiness, the increase of humility our study, we may find that we have been delighting in beautiful thoughts and feelings, in solemn acts of consecration and faith, while the only sure mark of the presence of God, the disappearance of self, was all the time wanting. Come and let us flee to Jesus, and hide ourselves in Him until we be clothed upon with His humility. That alone is our holiness.

Humility and Sin

'Sinners, of whom I am chief.' —1 TIM. i. 15

HUMILITY is often identified with penitence and contrition. As a consequence, there appears to be no way of fostering humility but by keeping the soul occupied with its sin. We have learned, I think, that humility is something else and something more. We have seen in the teaching of our Lord Jesus and the Epistles how often the virtue is inculcated without any reference to sin. In the very nature of things, in the whole relation of the creature to the Creator, in the life of Jesus as He lived it and imparts it to us, humility is the very essence of holiness as of blessedness. It is the displacement of self by the enthronement of God. Where God is all, self is nothing.

But though it is this aspect of the truth I have felt it specially needful to press, I need scarce say what new depth and intensity man's sin and God's grace give to the humility of the saints. We have only to look at a man like the Apostle Paul, to see how, through his life as a ransomed and a holy man, the deep consciousness of having been a sinner lives inextinguishably. We all know the passages in which he refers to his life as a persecutor and blasphemer. 'I am *the least of the apostles*, that am *not worthy to be called an apostle*, because I persecuted the Church of God.... I labored more abundantly than they all; yet not I, but the grace of God which was with me' (1 Cor. xv. 9,10). 'Unto me, who am *less than the least of all saints,* was this grace given, to preach to the heathen' (Eph. iii. 8). 'I was before a *blasphemer, and a persecutor, and injurious;* howbeit I obtained mercy, because I did it ignorantly in unbelief.... Christ Jesus came into the world to save *sinners, of whom I am chief*' (1 Tim. i. 13, 15). God's grace had saved him; God remembered his sins no more for ever; but never, never could he forget how terribly he had sinned. The more he rejoiced in God's salvation, and the more his experience of God's grace filled him with joy unspeakable, the clearer was his consciousness that he was a saved sinner, and that salvation had no meaning or sweetness except as the sense of his being a sinner made it precious and real to him. Never for a moment could he forget that it was a sinner God had taken up in His arms and crowned with His love.

The texts we have just quoted are often appealed to as Paul's confession of daily sinning. One has only to read them carefully in their connection, to see how little this is the case. They have a far deeper meaning, they refer to that which lasts throughout eternity, and which will give its deep undertone of amazement and adoration to the humility with which the ransomed bow before the throne, as those who have been washed from their sins in the blood of the Lamb. Never, never, even in, glory, can they be other than ransomed sinners; never for a moment in this life can God's child live in the full light of His love, but as he feels that the sin, out of which he has been saved, is his one only right and title to all that grace has promised to do. The humility with which first he came as a sinner, acquires a new meaning when he learns how it becomes him as a creature. And then ever again, the humility, in which he was born as a creature, has its deepest, richest tones of adoration, in the memory of what it is to be a monument of God's wondrous redeeming love.

The true import of what these expressions of St. Paul teach us comes out all the more strongly when we notice the remarkable fact that, through his whole Christian course, we never find from his pen, even in those epistles in which we have the most intensely personal unbosomings, anything like confession of sin. Nowhere is there any mention of shortcoming or defect, nowhere any suggestion to his readers that he has failed in duty, or sinned against the law of perfect love. On the contrary, there are passages not a few in which he vindicates himself in language that means nothing if it does not appeal to a faultless life before God and men. 'Ye are witnesses, and God also, how holily, and righteously, and unblameably we behaved ourselves toward you' (1 Thess. ii. 10). 'Our glorying is this, the testimony of our conscience, that in holiness and sincerity of God we behaved ourselves in the world, and more abundantly to you ward' (2 Cor. i. 12). This is not an ideal or an aspiration; it is an appeal to what his actual life had been. However we may account for this absence of confession of sin, all will admit that it must point to a life in the power of the Holy Ghost, such as is but seldom realized or expected in these our days.

The point which I wish to emphasize is this—that the very fact of the absence of such confession of sinning only gives the more force to the truth that it is not in daily sinning that the secret of the deeper humility will be found, but in the habitual, never for a moment to be forgotten position, which just the more abundant grace will keep more distinctly alive, that our only place, the only place of blessing, our one abiding position before God, must be that of those whose highest joy it is to confess that they are sinners saved by grace.

With Paul's deep remembrance of having sinned so terribly in the past, ere grace had met him, and the consciousness of being kept from present sinning, there was ever coupled the abiding remembrance of the dark hidden power of sin ever ready to come in, and only kept out by the presence and power of the indwelling Christ. 'In me, that is, in my flesh, dwelleth no good thing;' —these words of Rom. vii. describe the flesh as it is to the end. The glorious deliverance of Rom. viii. —'The law of the Spirit of life in Christ Jesus hath now made me free from the law of sin, which once led me captive' —is neither the annihilation nor the sanctification of the flesh, but a continuous victory given by the Spirit as He mortifies the deeds of the body. As health expels disease, and light swallows up darkness, and life conquers death, the indwelling of Christ through the Spirit is the health and light and life of the soul. But with this, the conviction of helplessness and danger ever tempers the faith in the momentary and unbroken action of the Holy Spirit into that chastened sense of dependence which makes the highest faith and joy the handmaids of a humility that only lives by the grace of God.

The three passages above quoted all show that it was the wonderful grace bestowed upon Paul, and of which he felt the need every moment, that humbled him so deeply. The grace of God that was with him, and enabled him to labor more abundantly than they all; the grace to preach to the heathen the unsearchable riches of Christ; the grace that was exceeding abundant with faith and love which is in Christ Jesus, —it was this grace of which it is the very nature and glory that it is for sinners, that kept the consciousness of his having once sinned, and being liable to sin, so intensely alive. 'Where sin abounded, grace did abound more exceedingly.' This reveals how the very essence of grace is to deal with and take away sin, and how it must ever be the more abundant the experience of grace, the more intense the consciousness of being a sinner. It is not sin, but God's grace showing a man and ever reminding him what a sinner he was, that, will keep him truly humble. It is not sin, but grace, that will make me indeed know myself a sinner, and make the sinner's place of deepest self-abasement the place I never leave.

I fear that there are not a few who, by strong expressions of self-condemnation and self-denunciation, have sought to humble themselves, and have to confess with sorrow that a humble spirit, a 'heart of humility,' with its accompaniments of kindness and compassion, of meekness and forbearance, is still as far off as ever. Being occupied with self, even amid the deepest self-abhorrence, can never free us from self. It is the revelation of God, not only by the law condemning sin but by His grace delivering from it, that will make us humble. The law may break the heart with fear; it is only grace that works that sweet humility which becomes a joy to the soul as its second nature. It was the revelation of God in His holiness, drawing nigh to make Himself known in His grace, that made Abraham and Jacob, Job and Isaiah, bow so low. It is the soul in which God the Creator, as the All of the creature in its nothingness, God the Redeemer in His grace, as the All of the sinner in his sinfulness, is waited for and trusted and worshipped, that will find itself so filled with His presence, that there will be no place for self. So alone can the promise be fulfilled: 'The haughtiness of man shall be brought low, and the Lord alone be exalted in that day.'

It is the sinner dwelling in the full light of God's holy, redeeming love, in the experience of that full indwelling of divine love, which comes through Christ and the Holy Spirit, who cannot but be humble. Not to be occupied with thy sin, but to be occupied with God, brings deliverance from self.

Humility and Faith

'How can ye believe, which receive glory from one another, and the glory that cometh from the only God ye seek not?' JOHN v. 44.

In an address I lately heard, the speaker said that the blessings of the higher Christian life were often like the objects exposed in a shop window, —one could see them clearly and yet could not reach them. If told to stretch out his hand and take, a man would answer, I cannot; there is a thick pane of plate-glass between me and them. And even so Christians may see clearly the blessed promises of perfect peace and rest, of overflowing love and joy, of abiding communion and fruitfulness, and yet feel that there was something between hindering the true possession. And what might that be? *Nothing but pride.* The promises made to faith are so free and sure; the invitations and encouragements so strong; the mighty power of God on which it may count is so near and free, —that it can only be something that hinders faith that hinders the blessing being ours. In our text Jesus discovers to us that it is indeed pride that makes faith impossible. 'How can ye believe, which receive glory from one another?' As we see how in their very nature pride and faith are irreconcilably at variance, we shall learn that faith and humility are at root one, and that we never can have more of true faith than we have of true humility; we shall see that we may indeed have strong intellectual conviction and assurance of the truth while pride is kept in the heart, but that it makes the living faith, which has power with God, an impossibility.

We need only think for a moment what faith is. Is it not the confession of nothingness and helplessness, the surrender and the waiting to let God work? Is it not in itself the most humbling thing there can be, —the acceptance of our place as dependents, who can claim or get or do nothing but what grace bestows? Humility is 'simply the disposition which prepares the soul for living on trust. And every, even the most secret breathing of pride, in self-seeking, self-will, self-confidence, or self-exaltation, is just the strengthening of that self which cannot enter the kingdom, or possess the things of the kingdom, because it refuses to allow God to be what He is and must be there—the All in All.

Faith is the organ or sense for the perception and apprehension of the heavenly world and its blessings. Faith seeks the glory that comes from God, that only comes where God is All. As long as we take glory from one another, as long as ever we seek and love and jealously guard the glory of this life, the honor and reputation that comes from men, we do not seek, and cannot receive the glory that comes from God. Pride renders faith impossible. Salvation comes through a cross and a crucified Christ. Salvation is the fellowship with the crucified Christ in the Spirit of His cross. Salvation is union with and delight in, salvation is participation in, the humility of Jesus. Is it wonder that our faith is so feeble when pride still reigns so much, and we have scarce learnt even to long or pray for humility as the most needful and blessed part of salvation?

Humility and faith are more nearly allied in Scripture than many know. See it in the life of Christ. There are two cases in which He spoke of a great faith. Had not the centurion, at whose faith He marveled, saying, 'I have not found so great faith, no, not in Israel!' spoken, *'I am not worthy* that Thou shouldst come under my roof'? And had not the mother to whom He spoke, 'O woman, great is thy faith!' accepted the name of dog, and said, *'Yea, Lord, yet the dogs eat of the crumbs'?* It is the humility that brings a soul to be nothing before God, that also removes every hindrance to faith, and makes it only fear lest it should dishonor Him by not trusting Him wholly.

Brother, have we not here the cause of failure in the pursuit of holiness? Is it not this, though we knew it not, that made our consecration and our faith so superficial and so short-lived? We had no idea to what an extent pride and self were still secretly working within us, and how alone God by His incoming and His mighty power could cast them out. We understood not how nothing but the new and divine nature, taking entirely the place of the old self, could make us really humble. We knew not that absolute, unceasing, universal humility must be the root-disposition of every prayer and every approach to God as well as of every dealing with man; and that we might as well attempt to see without eyes, or live without breath, as believe or draw nigh to God or dwell in His love, without an all-pervading humility and lowliness of heart.

Brother, have we not been making a mistake in taking so much trouble to believe, while all the time there was the old self in its pride seeking to possess itself of God's blessing and riches? No wonder we could not believe. Let us change our course. Let us seek first of all to humble ourselves under the mighty hand of God: *He will exalt us.* The cross, and the death, and the grave, into which Jesus humbled Himself, were His path to the glory of God. And they are our path. Let our one desire and our fervent prayer be, to be humbled with Him and like Him; let us accept gladly whatever can humble us before God or men;—this alone is the path to the glory of God.

You perhaps feel inclined to ask a question. I have spoken of some who have blessed experiences, or are the means of bringing blessing to others, and yet are lacking in humility. You ask whether these do not prove that they have true, even strong faith, though they show too clearly that they still seek too much the honor that cometh from men. There is more than one answer can be given. But the principal answer in our present connection is this: They indeed have a measure of faith, in proportion to which, with the special gifts bestowed upon them, is the blessing they bring to others. But in that very blessing the work of their faith is hindered, through the lack of humility. The blessing is often superficial or transitory, just because they are not the nothing that opens the way for God to be all. A deeper humility would without doubt bring a deeper and fuller blessing. The Holy Spirit not only working in them as a Spirit of power, but dwelling in them in the fullness of His grace, and specially that of humility, would through them communicate Himself to these converts for a life of power and holiness and steadfastness now all too little seen.

'How can ye believe, which receive glory from one another?' Brother! nothing can cure you of the desire of receiving glory from men, or of the sensitiveness and pain and anger which come when it is not given, but giving yourself to seek only the glory that comes from God. Let the glory of the All-glorious God be everything to you. You will be freed from the glory of men and of self, and be content and glad to be nothing. Out of this nothingness you will grow strong in faith, giving glory to God, and you will find that the deeper you sink in humility before Him, the nearer He is to fulfil the every desire of your faith.

Humility and Death to Self

'He humbled Himself and became obedient unto death.' —PHIL. ii. 8.

HUMILITY is the path to death, because in death it gives the highest proof of its perfection. Humility is the blossom of which death to self is the perfect fruit. Jesus humbled Himself unto death, and opened the path in which we too must walk. As there was no way for Him to prove His surrender to God to the very uttermost, or to give up and rise out of our human nature to the glory of the Father but through death, so with us too. Humility must lead us to die to self: so we prove how wholly we have given ourselves up to it and to God; so alone we are freed from fallen nature, and find the path that leads to life in God, to that full birth of the new nature, of which humility is the breath and the joy.

We have spoken of what Jesus did for His disciples when He communicated His resurrection life to them, when in the descent of the Holy Spirit He, the glorified and enthroned Meekness, actually came from heaven Himself to dwell in them. He won the power to do this through death: in its inmost nature the life He imparted was a life out of death, a life that had been surrendered to death, and been won through death. He who came to dwell in them was Himself One who had been dead and now lives for evermore. His life, His person, His presence, bears the marks of death, of being a life begotten out of death. That life in His disciples ever bears the death-marks too; it is only as the Spirit of the death, of the dying One, dwells and works in the soul, that the power of His life can be known. The first and chief of the marks of the dying of the Lord Jesus, of the death-marks that show the true follower of Jesus, is humility. For these two reasons: Only humility leads to perfect death; Only death perfects humility. Humility and death are in their very nature one: humility is the bud; in death the fruit is ripened to perfection.

Humility leads to perfect death. —Humility means the giving up of self and the taking of the place of perfect nothingness before God. Jesus humbled Himself, and became obedient unto death. In death He gave the highest, the perfect proof of having given up His will to the will of God. In death He gave up His self, with its natural reluctance to drink the cup; He gave up the life He had in union with our human nature; He died to self, and the sin that tempted Him; so, as man, He entered into the perfect life of God. If it had not been for His boundless humility, counting Himself as nothing except as a servant to do and suffer the will of God, He never would have died.

This gives us the answer to the question so often asked, and of which the meaning is so seldom clearly apprehended: How can I die to self? The death to self is not your work, it is God's work. In Christ *you are dead* to sin the life there is in you has gone through the process of death and resurrection; you may be sure you are indeed dead to sin. But the full manifestation of the power of this death in your disposition and conduct, depends upon the measure in which the Holy Spirit imparts the power of the death of Christ And here it is that the teaching is needed: if you would enter into full fellowship with Christ in His death, and know the full deliverance from self, humble yourself. This is your one duty. Place yourself before God in your utter helplessness; consent heartily to the fact of your impotence to slay or make alive yourself; sink down into your own nothingness, in the spirit of meek and patient and trustful surrender to God. Accept every humiliation, look upon every fellow-man who tries or vexes you, as a means of grace to humble you. Use every opportunity of humbling yourself before your fellow-men as a help to abide humble before God. God will accept such humbling of yourself as the proof that your whole heart desires it, as the very best prayer for it, as your preparation for His mighty work of grace, when, by the mighty strengthening of His Holy Spirit, He reveals Christ fully in you, so that He, in His form of a servant, is truly formed in you, and dwells in your heart. It is the path of humility which leads to perfect death, the full and perfect experience that we are dead in Christ.

Then follows: *Only this death leads to perfect humility.* Oh, beware of the mistake so many make, who would fain be humble, but are afraid to be too humble. They have so many qualifications and limitations, so many reasonings and questionings, as to what true humility is to be and to do, that they never unreservedly yield themselves to it. Beware of this. Humble yourself unto the death. It is in the death to self that humility is perfected. Be sure that at the root of all real experience of more grace, of all true advance in consecration, of all actually increasing conformity to the likeness of Jesus, there must be a deadness to self that proves itself to God and men in our dispositions and habits. It is sadly possible to speak of the death-life and the Spirit-walk, while even the tenderest love cannot but see how much there is of self. The death to self has no surer death-mark than a humility which makes itself of no reputation, which empties out itself, and takes the form of a servant. It is possible to speak much and honestly of fellowship with a despised and rejected Jesus, and of bearing His cross, while the meek and lowly, the kind and gentle humility of the Lamb of God is not seen, is scarcely sought. The Lamb of God means to two things—meekness and death. Let us seek to receive Him in both forms. In Him they are inseparable: they must be in us too.

What a hopeless task if we had to do the work! Nature never can overcome nature, not even with the help of grace. Self can never cast out self, even in the regenerate man. Praise God! the work has been done, and finished and perfected for ever. The death of Jesus, once and forever, is our death to self. And the ascension of Jesus, His entering once and for ever into the Holiest, has given us the Holy Spirit to communicate to us in power, and make our very own, the power of the death-life. As the soul, in the pursuit and practice of humility, follows in the steps of Jesus, its consciousness of the need of something more is awakened, its desire and hope is quickened, its faith is strengthened, and it learns to look up and claim and receive that true fullness of the Spirit of Jesus, which can daily maintain His death to self and sin in its full power, and make humility the all pervading spirit of our life.[5]

---

[5] 'To die to self, or come from under its power, is not, cannot be done, by any active resistance we can make to it by the powers of nature. The one true way of dying to self is the way of patience, meekness, humility, and resignation to God. This is the truth and perfection of dying to self.... For if I ask you what the Lamb of God means, must you not tell me that it is and means the perfection of patience, meekness, humility, and resignation to God? Must you not therefore say that a desire and faith of these virtues is an application to Christ, is a giving up yourself to Him and the perfection of faith in Him? And then, because

'Are ye ignorant that all we who were baptized into Jesus Christ were *baptized into His death?* Reckon yourselves to be *dead unto sin,* but alive unto God in Christ Jesus. Present yourself unto God, as *alive from the dead.'* The whole self consciousness of the Christian is to be imbued and characterized by the spirit that animated the death of Christ. He has ever to present himself to God as one who has died in Christ, and in Christ is alive from the dead, bearing about in his body the dying of the Lord Jesus. His life ever bears the two-fold mark: its roots striking in true humility deep into the grave of Jesus, the death to sin and self; its head lifted up in resurrection power to the heaven where Jesus is.

Believer, claim in faith the death and the life of Jesus as thine. Enter in His grave into the rest from self and its work—the rest of God. With Christ, who committed His spirit into the Father's hands, humble thyself and descend each day into that perfect, helpless dependence upon God. God will raise thee up and exalt thee. Sink every morning in deep, deep nothingness into the grave of Jesus; every day the life of Jesus will be manifest in thee, Let a willing, loving, restful, happy humility be the mark that thou hast indeed claimed thy birthright—the baptism into the death of Christ. 'By one offering He has perfected for ever them that are sanctified.' The souls that enter into *His* humiliation will find *in Him* the power to see and count self dead, and, as those who have learned and received of Him, to walk with all lowliness and meekness, forbearing one another in love. The death-life is seen in a meekness and lowliness like that of Christ.

Humility and Happiness

'Most gladly therefore will I rather glory in my weaknesses, that the strength of Christ may rest upon me. Wherefore I take pleasure in weakness: for when I am weak then am I strong.'—2 COR. xii. 9. 10.

LEST Paul should exalt himself, by reason of the exceeding greatness of the revelations, a thorn in the flesh was sent him to keep him humble. Paul's first desire was to have it removed, and he besought the Lord thrice that it might depart. The answer came that the trial was a blessing; that, in the weakness and humiliation it brought, the grace and strength of the Lord could be the better manifested. Paul at once entered upon a new stage in his relation to the trial: instead of simply

---

this inclination of your heart to sink down in patience, meekness, humility, and resignation to God, is truly giving up all that you are and all that you have from fallen Adam, it is perfectly leaving all you have to follow Christ; it is your highest act of faith in Him. Christ is nowhere but in these virtues; when they are there, He is in His own kingdom. Let this be the Christ you follow.

'The Spirit of divine love can have no birth in any fallen creature, till it wills and chooses to be dead to all self, in a patient, humble resignation to the power and mercy of God.

'I seek for all my salvation through the merits and mediation of the meek, humble, patient, suffering Lamb of God, who alone hath power to bring forth the blessed birth of these heavenly virtues in my soul. There is no possibility of salvation but in and by the birth of the meek, humble, patient, resigned Lamb of God in our souls. When the Lamb of God hath brought forth a real birth of His own meekness, humility, and full resignation to God in our souls, then it is the birthday of the Spirit of love in our souls, which, whenever we attain, will feast our souls with such peace and joy in God as will blot out the remembrance of everything that we called peace or joy before.

'This way to God is infallible. This infallibility is grounded in the twofold character of our Savior: 1. As He is the Lamb of God, a principle of all meekness and humility in the soul; 2. As He is the Light of heaven, and blesses eternal nature, and turns it into a kingdom of heaven, —when we are willing to get rest to our souls in meek, humble resignation to God, then it is that He, as the Light of God and heaven, joyfully breaks in upon us, turns our darkness into light, and begins that kingdom of God and of love within us, which will never have an end.' —See Wholly For God, pp 84-102. (The whole passage deserves careful study, showing most remarkably how the continual sinking down in humility before God is, from man's side, the only way to die to self. The whole dialogue has been published separately under the title Dying to Self: A Golden Dialogue. By William Law. With Notes by A.M., Nisbet & Co. Everyone who would study and practice humility will find in this golden dialogue what it is that hinders our humility, how we are to be delivered from it, and what the blessing of the Spirit of Love is that comes to the humble from Christ, the meek and lowly Lamb of God.

enduring it, *he most gladly gloried* in it; instead of asking for deliverance, *he took pleasure* in it. He had learned that the place of humiliation is the place of blessing, of power, of joy.

Every Christian virtually passes through these two stages in his pursuit of humility. In the first he fears and flees and seeks deliverance from all that can humble him. He has not yet learnt to seek humility at any cost. He has accepted the command to be humble, and seeks to obey it, though only to find how utterly he fails. He prays for humility, at times very earnestly; but in his secret heart he prays more, if not in word, then in wish, to be kept from the very things that will make him humble. He is not yet so in love with humility as the beauty of the Lamb of God, and the joy of heaven, that he would sell all to procure it. In his pursuit of it, and his prayer for it, there is still somewhat of a sense of burden and of bondage; to humble himself has not yet become the spontaneous expression of a life and a nature that is essentially humble. It has not yet become his joy and only pleasure. He cannot yet say, 'Most gladly do I glory in weakness, I take pleasure in whatever humbles me.'

But can we hope to reach the stage in which this will be the case? Undoubtedly. And what will it be that brings us there? *That* which brought Paul there—*a new revelation of the Lord Jesus.* Nothing but the presence of God can reveal and expel self. A clearer insight was to be given to Paul into the deep truth that the presence of Jesus will banish every desire to seek anything in ourselves, and will make us delight in every humiliation that prepares us for His fuller manifestation. Our humiliations lead us, in the experience of the presence and power of Jesus, to choose humility as our highest blessing. Let us try to learn the lessons the story of Paul teaches us.

We may have advanced believers, eminent teachers, men of heavenly experiences, who have not yet fully learnt the lesson of perfect humility, gladly glorying in weakness. We see this in Paul. The danger of exalting himself was coming very near. He knew not yet perfectly what it was to be nothing; to die, that Christ alone might live in him; to take pleasure in all that brought him low. It appears as if this were the highest lesson that he had to learn, full conformity to his Lord in that self-emptying where he gloried in weakness that God might be all.

The highest lesson a believer has to learn is humility. Oh that every Christian who seek to advance in holiness may remember this well! There may be intense consecration, and fervent zeal and heavenly experience, and yet, if it is not prevented by very special dealings of the Lord, there may be an unconscious self-exaltation with it all. Let us learn the lesson, —the highest holiness is the deepest humility; and let us remember that comes not of itself, but only as it is made matter of special dealing on the part of our faithful Lord and His faithful servant.

Let us look at our lives in the light of this experience, and see whether we gladly glory in weakness, whether we take pleasure, as Paul did, in injuries, in necessities, in distresses. Yes, let us ask whether we have learnt to regard a reproof, just or unjust, a reproach from friend or enemy, an injury, or trouble, or difficulty into which others bring us, as above all an opportunity of proving Jesus is all to us, how our own pleasure or honor are nothing, and how humiliation is in very truth what we take pleasure in. It is indeed blessed, the deep happiness of heaven, to be so free from self that whatever is said of us or done to us is lost and swallowed up, in the thought that Jesus is all.

Let us trust Him who took charge of Paul to take charge of us too. Paul needed special discipline, and with it special instruction, to learn, what was more precious than even the unutterable things he had heard in heaven—what it is to glory in weakness and lowliness. We need it, too, oh so much. He who cared for him will care for us too. He watches over us with a jealous, loving care, 'lest we exalt ourselves'. When we are doing so, He seeks to discover to us the evil, and deliver us from it. In trial and weakness and trouble He seeks to bring us low, until we so learn that His grace is all, as to take pleasure in the very thing that brings us and keeps us low. His strength made perfect in our weakness, His presence filling and satisfying our emptiness, becomes the secret of a humility that need never fail. It can, as Paul, in full sight of what God works in us, and through us, ever say, 'In nothing was I behind the chiefest apostles, *though I am nothing.'* His humiliations had led him to true humility, with its wonderful gladness and glorying and pleasure in all that humbles.

'Most gladly will I glory in my weaknesses, that the power of Christ may rest upon me; wherefore I take pleasure in weaknesses. 'The humble man has learnt the secret of abiding gladness. The weaker he feels, the lower he sinks; the greater his humiliations appear, the more the power and the presence of Christ are his portion, until, as he says, 'I am nothing,' the word of his Lord brings ever deeper joy: 'My grace is sufficient for thee.'

I feel as if I must once again gather up all in the two lessons: the danger of pride is greater and nearer than we think, and the grace for humility too.

The danger of pride is greater and nearer than we think, and that especially at the time of our highest experiences. The preacher of spiritual truth with an admiring congregation hanging on his lips, the gifted speaker on a Holiness platform expounding the secrets of the heavenly life, the Christian giving testimony to a blessed experience, the evangelist moving on as in triumph, and made a blessing to rejoicing multitudes, —no man knows the hidden, the unconscious danger to which these are exposed. Paul was in danger without knowing it; what Jesus did for him is written for our admonition, that we may know our danger and know our only safety. If ever it has been said of a teacher or professor of holiness, —he is so full of self; or, he does not practice what he preaches; or, his blessing has not made him humbler or gentler, —let it be said no more. Jesus, in whom we trust, can make us humble.

Yes, the grace for humility is greater and nearer, too, than we think. The humility of Jesus is our salvation: Jesus Himself is our humility. Our humility is His care and His work. His grace is sufficient for us, to meet the temptation of pride too. His strength will be perfected in our weakness. Let us choose to be weak, to be low, to be nothing. Let humility be to us joy and gladness. Let us gladly glory and take pleasure in weakness, in all that can humble us and keep us low; the power of Christ will rest upon us. Christ humbled Himself, therefore God exalted Him. Christ will humble us, and keep us humble; let us heartily consent, let us trustfully and joyfully accept all that humbles; the power of Christ will rest upon us. We shall find that the deepest humility is the secret of the truest happiness, of a joy that nothing can destroy.

Humility and Exaltation

'He that humbleth himself shall be exalted.'—LUKE xiv. 11, xviii. 13.

'God giveth grace to the humble. Humble yourself in the sight of the Lord, and He shall exalt you.'—JAS. iv. 10.

'Humble yourselves therefore under the mighty hand of God, that He may exalt you in due time.'—1 PET. v. 6.

JUST yesterday I was asked the question, How am I to conquer this pride? The answer; was simple. Two things are needed. Do what; God says is your work: humble yourself. Trust Him to do what He says is His work: He will exalt you.

The command is clear: humble yourself. That does not mean that it is your work to conquer and cast out the pride of your nature, and to form within yourself the lowliness of the holy Jesus. No, this is God's work; the very essence of that exaltation, wherein He lifts you up into the real likeness of the beloved Son. What the command does mean is this: take every opportunity of humbling yourself before God and man. In the faith of the grace that is already working in you; in the assurance of the more grace for victory that is coming; up to the light that conscience each time flashes upon the pride of the heart and its workings; notwithstanding all there may be of failure and falling, stand persistently as under the unchanging command: humble yourself. Accept with gratitude everything that God allows from within or without, from friend or enemy, in nature or in grace, to remind you of your need of humbling, and to help you to it. Reckon humility to be indeed the mother-virtue, your very first duty before God, the one perpetual safeguard of the soul, and set your heart upon it as the source of all blessing. The promise is divine and sure: He that humbleth himself shall be exalted. See that you do the one thing God asks: humble yourself. God will see that does the one thing He has promised. He will give more grace; He will exalt you in due time.

All God's dealings with man are characterized by two stages. There is the time of preparation, when command and promise, with the mingled experience of effort and impotence, of failure and partial success, with the holy expectancy of something better which these waken, train and discipline men for a higher stage. Then comes the time of fulfilment, when faith inherits the promise, and enjoys what it had so often struggled for in vain. This law holds good in every part of the Christian life, and in the pursuit of every separate virtue. And that because it is grounded in the very nature of things. In all that concerns our redemption, God must needs take the initiative. When that has been done, man's turn comes. In the effort after obedience and attainment, he must learn to know his impotence, in self-despair to die to himself, and so be fitted voluntarily and intelligently to receive from God the end, the completion of that of which he had accepted the beginning in ignorance. So, God who had been the Beginning, ere man rightly knew Him, or fully understood what His purpose was, is longed for and welcomed as the End, as the All in All.

It is even thus, too, in the pursuit of humility. To every Christian the command comes from the throne of God Himself: humble yourself. The earnest attempt to listen and obey will be rewarded—yes, rewarded—with the painful discovery of two things. The one, what depth of pride, that is of unwillingness to count oneself and to be counted nothing, to submit absolutely to God, there was, that one never knew. The other, what utter impotence there is in all our efforts, and in all our prayers too for God's help, to destroy the hideous monster. Blessed the man who now learns to put his hope in God, and to persevere, notwithstanding all the power of pride within him, in acts of humiliation before God and Men. We know the law of human nature: acts produce habits, habits breed dispositions, dispositions form the will, and the rightly-formed will is character. It is no otherwise in the work of grace. As acts, persistently repeated, beget habits and dispositions, and these strengthened the will, He who works both to will and to do comes with His mighty power and Spirit; and the humbling of the proud heart with which the' penitent saint cast himself so often before God, is rewarded with the 'more grace' of the humble heart, in which the Spirit of Jesus has conquered, and brought the new nature to its maturity, and He the meek and lowly One now dwells for ever.

Humble yourselves in the sight of the Lord, and He will exalt you. And wherein does the exaltation consist? The highest glory of the creature is in being only a vessel, to receive and enjoy and show forth the glory of God. It can do this only as it is willing to be nothing in itself, that God may be all. Water always fills first the lowest places. The lower, the emptier a man lies before God, the speedier and the fuller will be the inflow of the divine glory. The exaltation God promises is not, cannot be, any external thing apart from Himself: all that He has to give or can give is only more of Himself, Himself to take more complete possession. The exaltation is not, like an earthly prize, something arbitrary, in no necessary connection with the conduct to be rewarded. No, but it is in its very nature the effect and result of the humbling of ourselves. It is nothing but the gift of such a divine indwelling humility, such a conformity to and possession of the humility of the Lamb of God, as fits us for receiving fully the indwelling of God.

He that humbleth himself shall be exalted. Of the truth of these words Jesus Himself is the proof; of the certainty of their fulfilment to us He is the pledge. Let us take His yoke upon us and learn of Him, for He is meek and lowly of heart. If we are but willing to stoop to Him, as He has stooped to us, He will yet stoop to each one of us again, and we shall find ourselves not unequally yoked with Him. As we enter deeper into the fellowship of His humiliation, and either humble ourselves or bear the humbling of men, we can count upon it that the Spirit of His exaltation, 'the Spirit of God and of glory,' will rest upon us. The presence and the power of the glorified Christ will come to them that are of an humble spirit. When God can again have His rightful place in us, He will lift us up. Make His glory thy care in humbling thyself; He will make thy glory His care in perfecting thy humility, and breathing into thee, as thy abiding life, the very Spirit of His Son. As the all-pervading life of God possesses thee, there will be nothing so natural, and nothing so sweet, as to be nothing, with not a thought or wish for self, because all is occupied with Him who filleth all. 'Most gladly will I glory in my weakness, that the strength of Christ may rest upon me.'

Brother, have we not here the reason that our consecration and our faith have availed so little in the pursuit of holiness? It was by self and its strength that the work was done under the name of faith; it was for self and its happiness that God was called in; it was, unconsciously, but still truly, in self and its holiness that the soul rejoiced. We never knew that humility, absolute, abiding, Christlike humility and self-effacement, pervading and marking our whole life with God and man, was the most essential element of the life of the holiness we sought for.

It is only in the possession of God that I lose myself. As it is in the height and breadth and glory of the sunshine that the littleness of the mote playing in its beams is seen, even so humility is the taking our place in God's presence to be nothing but a mote dwelling in the sunlight of His love.

'How great is God! how small am I!
Lost, swallowed up in Love's immensity!
God only there, not I.'

May God teach us to believe that to be humble, to be nothing in His presence, is the highest attainment, and the fullest blessing of the Christian life. He speaks to us: 'I dwell in the high and holy place, and with him the is of a contrite and humble spirit.' Be this our portion!

'Oh, to be emptier, lowlier,
Mean, unnoticed, and unknown,
And to God a vessel holier,
Filled with Christ, and Christ alone!'

Endnote

A Secret of Secrets: Humility the Soul of True Prayer. —Till the spirit of the heart be renewed, till it is emptied of all earthly desires, and stands in an habitual hunger and thirst after God, which is the true spirit of prayer; till then, all our prayer will be, more or less, but too much like lessons given to scholars; and we shall mostly say them, only because we dare not neglect them. But be not discouraged; take the following advice, and then you may go to church without any danger of mere lip-labor or hypocrisy, although there should be a hymn or a prayer, whose language is higher than that of your heart. Do this: go to the church as the publican went to the temple; stand inwardly in the spirit of your mind in that form which he outwardly expressed, when he cast down his eyes, and could only say, 'God be merciful to me, a sinner.' Stand unchangeably, at least in your desire, in this form or state of heart; it will sanctify every petition that comes out of your mouth; and when anything is read or sung or prayed, that is more exalted than your heart is, if you make this an occasion of further sinking down in the spirit of the publican, you will then be helped, and highly blessed, by those prayers and praises which seem only to belong to a heart better than yours.

This, my friend, is a secret of secrets; it will help you to reap where you have not sown, and be a continual source of grace in your soul; for everything that inwardly stirs in you, or outwardly happens to you, becomes a real good to you, if it finds or excites in you this humble state of mind. For nothing is in vain, or without profit to the humble soul; it stands always in a state of divine growth; everything that falls upon it is like a dew of heaven to it. Shut up yourself, therefore, in this form of Humility; all good is enclosed in it; it is a water of heaven, that turns the fire of the fallen soul into the meekness of the divine life, and creates that oil, out of which the love to God and man gets its flame. Be enclosed, therefore, always in it; let it be as a garment wherewith you are always covered, and a girdle with which you are girt; breathe nothing but in and from its spirit; see nothing but with its eyes; hear nothing but with its ears. And then, whether you are in the church or out of the church, hearing the praises of God or receiving wrongs from men and the world, all will be edification, and everything will help forward your growth in the life of God. —*The Spirit of Prayer,* Pt. II. p. 121.

A Prayer for Humility

I will here give you an infallible touchstone, that will try all to the truth. It is this: retire from the world and all conversation, only for one month; neither write, nor read, nor debate anything with yourself; stop all the former workings of your heart and mind: and, with all the strength of your heart, stand all this month, as continually as you can, in the following form of prayer to God. Offer it frequently on your knees; but whether sitting, walking, or standing, be always inwardly longing, and earnestly praying this one prayer to God: 'That of His great goodness He would make known to you, and take from your heart, *every kind and form and degree of Pride,* whether it be from evil spirits, or your own corrupt nature; and that He would awaken in you the *deepest depth and truth of that Humility,* which can make you capable of His light and Holy Spirit.' Reject every thought, but that of waiting and praying in this matter from the bottom of your heart, with such truth and earnestness, as people in torment wish to pray and be delivered from it.... If you can and will give yourself up in truth and sincerity to this spirit of prayer, I will venture to affirm that, if you had twice as many evil spirits in you as Mary Magdalene had, they will all be cast out of you, and you will be forced with her to weep tears of love at the feet of the holy Jesus. —*The Spirit of Prayer,* Pt. II. p. 124.

CPSIA information can be obtained
at www.ICGtesting.com
Printed in the USA
LVHW040148220423
745008LV00001B/61

9 781640 322233

Grundriß

der

Geschichte der Verfassung, Verwaltung und Gesetzgebung

des

Preußischen Staats

seit der Zeit des dreißigjährigen Krieges bis zum Jahre 1850.

Von

Silberschlag, Dr. jur.

Stadt- und Kreis-Richter.

Berlin.

Druck und Verlag von Georg Reimer.

1860.

Vorwort.

Die Geschichte der Verfassung und Gesetzgebung des Preußischen Staats pflegt selbst von den Preußischen Juristen nur sehr wenig beachtet zu werden; was das übrige gebildete Publicum betrifft, so kann man dreist behaupten, daß dasselbe nicht bloß die Geschichte der Englischen oder Französischen Verfassung und Gesetzgebung, sondern auch die der Verfassuug von Rom oder Athen weit besser kennt, als die Geschichte der Verfassung und Gesetzgebung unseres Staates. Dennoch dürfte letztere schon um deswillen für jeden Freund unseres Vaterlandes von hohem Interesse sein, weil sich in ihr weit besser als in der eigentlich politischen Geschichte der frühere Culturzustand unserer Nation und die allmälig in demselben vorgegangene Veränderung erkennen läßt. Auch trägt wohl Nichts so sehr zu einer richtigen Beurtheilung der gegenwärtigen Rechtszustände bei als die Kenntniß der frühern Rechtszustände und der allmäligen Entwicklung der gegenwärtigen.

In dem engen Raum dieser Broschüre können wir freilich nur einen summarischen Ueberblick über das weite und bisher so wenig bearbeitete Feld der Geschichte der Preußischen Verfassung und Gesetzgebung geben; ob es uns gelungen sei, das Gesammtbild und den Geist der frühern Zustände richtig aufzufassen, müssen wir dem Urtheile eines jeden anheimstellen; die Richtigkeit der einzelnen von uns gemachten factischen Angaben dagegen wird verbürgt durch die benutzten Quellen. Es sind dies die officiellen Sammlungen der Gesetze unseres Vaterlandes, für die ältere Zeit die bekannten Sammluugen der Verordnungen von Rabe, Mylius, Korn, ferner Mülleri practica Marchica; in Bezug auf historische Angaben haben wir vorzugsweise die Geschichte Friedrichs II. von Preuß, von Orlich's Geschichte des großen Kurfürsten und Förster's Geschichte Friedrich Wilhelms I., sowie Pauly's Geschichte des Brandenburg-Preußischen Staats benutzt.

Wenn unsere Arbeit dazu beiträgt, das Interesse für die Geschichte der Preußischen Gesetzgebung zu beleben, so ist der Zweck des Verfassers erreicht.

Magdeburg, den 7. Mai 1860.

Inhalts-Verzeichniß.

§. 1. Verfassung der Mark Brandenburg vor dem dreißigjährigen Kriege. Große Beschränkung der Macht des Kurfürsten. . . . . S. 1
§. 2. Militärische Machtlosigkeit des Kurfürsten. . . . . — 3
§. 3. Das Criminal-Verfahren in der Mark während des 16. und 17. Jahrhunderts. . . . . — 6
§. 4. Die Mängel der ständischen Verfassung. . . . . — 9
§. 5. Erweiterung der landesherrlichen Gewalt in der Mark während des dreißigjährigen Krieges. Anwerbung eines stehenden Heeres durch Kurfürst Georg Wilhelm und den großen Kurfürsten. . — 10
§. 6. u. 7. Materielle Aufhebung der ständischen Verfassung im Herzogthum Preußen und den übrigen Landestheilen. . . . . — 13
§. 8. Die Verwaltungs-Behörden des Brandenburg-Preußischen Staats seit der Regierung des großen Kurfürsten. . . . . . . — 15
§. 9. Der Staatsrath. . . . . — 18
§. 10. Gerichts-Verfassung und Gerichts-Verfahren bis zur Regierung Friedrich Wilhelms I. . . . . — 20
§. 11. Reform des Criminal-Verfahrens unter Friedrich Wilhelm I. . — 22
§. 12. Cabinets-Justiz Friedrich Wilhelms I. Widerrechtliche Hinrichtung des Kriegs- und Domainen-Raths von Schlubuth. . . . . — 23
§. 13. Das materielle Strafrecht unter Friedrich Wilhelm I. . . . . — 25
§. 14. Die Rechts-Sicherheit im Preußischen Staate verglichen mit den Zuständen im übrigen Deutschland. . . . . — 26
§. 15. Die Armenpflege bis zum Ende des 17. Jahrhunderts. . . . — 27
§. 16. Reform derselben unter Friedrich I. und Friedrich Wilhelm I. und Einwirkung dieser Reform auf die öffentliche Sicherheit und Criminalrechtspflege. . . . . — 28
§. 17. Reformen Friedrichs II. a) in Bezug auf das Straf-Verfahren. — 30
§. 18. b) in Bezug auf das Criminalrecht. . . . . — 32
§. 19. Justiz-Reform des Ministers v. Cocceji. . . . . — 33
§. 20. Justiz-Reform des Ministers v. Carmer. . . . . — 36
§. 21. Anlaß zur Abfassung des Allgemeinen Land-Rechts. . . . . — 37

§. 22. Rückblick auf die Aenderungen des Rechtszustandes seit der Zeit des großen Kurfürsten: a) Standesvorrechte des Adels. . . — 38
§. 23. b) Gutsherrlich-bäuerliche Verhältnisse. . . . . — 39
§. 24. c) Allmälige Aufhebung der Leibeigenschaft. . . . . — 41
§. 25. Einzelne Aenderungen des Civilrechts während des 18. Jahrhunderts vor Abfassung des Land-Rechts. . . . . — 43
§. 26. Die Nothwendigkeit der Schriftform der Verträge. . . . . . — 44
§. 27. Das General-Land-Schulen-Reglement von 1763. . . . . . — 45
§. 28. Abfassung des Allgemeinen Land-Rechts. . . . . — 46
§. 29. u. 30. Die Haupt-Principien und einzelne Neuerungen desselben. — 47
§. 31. Militair-Gesetzgebung vom Ende des 17. Jahrhunderts bis 1806. — 52
§. 32. Steuern und Abgaben während des 18. Jahrhunderts. . . . — 54
§. 33. Das Mercantil-System in der Preußischen Gesetzgebung. . . . — 57
§. 34. Ueberblick über den Rechtszustand des Staats im Jahre 1806. — 58
§. 35. Vergleichung desselben a) mit den Zuständen Englands. . . . — 59
§. 36. b) mit den heutigen Zuständen Mecklenburgs. . . . . . . — 60
§. 37. u. 38. Reform des materiellen Rechts von 1806—1813. . . . — 62
§. 39. Neugestaltung der Militair- und Civil-Behörden. . . . . . — 64
§. 40. Reform der Militair-Gesetzgebung. . . . . — 66
§. 41. Reform der Steuergesetze. . . . . — 67
§. 42. u. 43. Ueber die Art der Einführung dieser Reformen. . . . — 67
§. 44. Die Haupturheber derselben. Das Vorbild der Westphälischen und Französischen Gesetzgebung. . . . . — 69
§. 45. Reorganisation des Staats im Jahre 1815. . . . . — 72
§. 46. Verfassung des Staats von 1815—1847. . . . . — 73
§. 47. u. 48. Der Beamten-Stand. Geist desselben. . . . . . . — 75
§. 49. Das Patent vom 3. Februar 1847 und die Verfassung vom 31. Januar 1850. . . . . — 76
§. 50. Principien derselben. . . . . — 78
§. 51. Verhältniß derselben zur Deutschen Bundes-Acte. . . . . . — 78
§. 52. Gegner der Verfassung. . . . . — 79
§. 53. Neuerungen derselben in Bezug auf Feststellung des Verhältnisses des Staats zur Kirche. Preßfreiheit. . . . . — 81
§. 54. Geschichte des Civilrechts von 1815—1850. Die Allgemeine Wechsel-Ordnung. . . . . — 83
§. 55. Einzelne Special-Gesetze. . . . . — 85
§. 56. Armen-Gesetze. . . . . — 87
§. 57. Das Criminal-Recht. . . . . — 89
§. 58. Aenderungen im Gerichts-Verfahren und der Gerichts-Verfassung. — 90
§. 59. Organisation der Verwaltungs-Behörden. Gemeinde-Verfassung. — 91
§. 60. Zoll-Gesetze. Der Zoll-Verein. . . . . — 94
§. 61. Directe Steuern. . . . . — 96
§. 62. Gegenwärtige Lage des Beamten-Standes. . . . . — 97
§. 63. Rückblick. . . . . —100

Die Geschichte der Verfassung des Brandenburg-Preußischen Staats seit dem Ende des Mittelalters bis zur neuesten Zeit zerfällt in zwei Haupt-Abschnitte. Der erste geht bis in die Zeit des dreißigjährigen Krieges. Bis dahin war die Verfassung eine aristokratisch-monarchische, in welcher die bevorrechteten Stände die Herrschaft mit einem äußerst eingeschränkten Monarchen theilten; von dieser Zeit an bildete sich die Verfassung rasch um in eine absolut-monarchische, in welcher die Stände bald nur noch eine nominelle Wirksamkeit hatten. Unter dieser absolut-monarchischen Regierungsform wurden namentlich durch die Gesetzgebung der Jahre 1806—1813 die hauptsächlichsten der alten kastenartigen Stände-Unterschiede und die noch bestehenden Reste der persönlichen Unfreiheit und Leibeigenschaft aufgehoben.

Die neueste Zeit sah endlich die Verwandlung der absolut-monarchischen Regierungs-Form in eine constitutionell-monarchische.

Um die innere Geschichte unseres Staates seit der Zeit des dreißigjährigen Krieges richtig zu verstehen, müssen wir einen Blick auf die Zustände werfen, welche bis zum dreißigjährigen Kriege in unserm Vaterlande bestanden.

§. 1.

Als der Kurfürst Friedrich I. von Hohenzollern mit der Mark beliehen war, kostete es ihm bekanntlich große Anstrengungen, die Huldigung des gesammten Adels der Mark zu erlangen. Es glückte ihm dies zuletzt hauptsächlich durch die Unterstützung der Märkischen Städte und der benachbarten Fürsten, welche durch die räuberische Ungebundenheit der Quitzows und anderer Märkischen Edelleute viel gelitten hatten. Etwa 100 Jahre später that Kurfürst Joachim I. einen sehr bedeutenden Schritt zur Begründung eines geordneten Rechts-Zustandes und zugleich zur Erweiterung der monarchischen Gewalt, indem er das Faustrecht aufhob, die Wegelagerungen der Edelleute mit eiserner Strenge unterdrückte, was ihm bekanntlich nicht ohne harten Kampf gelang, und indem er im Jahre 1516 in Gemeinschaft mit den Ständen das Kammergericht einsetzte.

Unter Kurfürst Joachim II. gewann hiernächst die landesherrliche Macht bei Einführung der Reformation an Ansehen, indem die bisher den katholischen Bischöfen zustehende Aufsicht über die niedere Geistlichkeit, sowie die geistliche Gerichtsbarkeit, namentlich in Ehe Sachen auf die landesherrlichen Consistorien überging.

Dennoch blieb die fürstliche Macht durch die Rechte der Stände im höchsten Grade beschränkt.

Diese letztern bestanden seit Einführung der Reformation nur aus den adlichen Gutsbesitzern und den Städten, sie hatten namentlich Theilnahme an der Gesetzgebung, so daß ohne ihre Zustimmung kein Gesetz erlassen werden konnte, und das Steuerbewilligungsrecht. Für den Fall eines Streits zwischen dem Kurfürsten und den Ständen stand den letztern ursprünglich das Recht der Berufung an den Kaiser zu; dies Recht fiel zwar dadurch hinweg, daß dem Kurfürsten im Jahre 1586 vom Kaiser Rudolph II. das privilegium de non appellando ertheilt wurde, jedoch war dies kaiserliche Privilegium, wie in demselben ausdrücklich gesagt ist, nur aus dem Grunde ertheilt, weil der Kurfürst sich den Ständen gegenüber verpflichtet hatte, alle zwischen ihm und denselben entstehenden Streitigkeiten einem Schiedsgericht zu unterwerfen, welches aus sechs zur Hälfte vom Kurfürsten und zur Hälfte von den Ständen zu ernennenden Personen bestehen sollte. Was die Gerichtsbarkeit und Polizei-Verwaltung betraf, so war dieselbe auf den landesherrlichen Domainen in der Regel in den Händen der vom Kurfürsten selbst ernannten Beamten, oft jedoch waren die Domainen auf Jahrzehnde in den Pfandbesitz adlicher Familien übergegangen, die dann Polizei-Verwaltung und Gerichtsbarkeit auf denselben ausübten.

Im Uebrigen, d. h. abgesehen von den Domainen, war auf dem Lande die Gerichtsbarkeit im Allgemeinen als Patrimonial-Gerichtsbarkeit in den Händen der adlichen Gutsbesitzer, welche auch die Polizei-Verwaltung hatten; in den Städten hatte fast immer der Rath als oberste städtische Behörde Gerichtsbarkeit und Polizei-Gewalt, auf die Zusammensetzung des Rathes aber, der sich meistens selbst ergänzte, hatte der Kurfürst nur in den wenigsten Städten entscheidenden Einfluß.

Allerdings standen nun die städtischen sowohl als die Patrimonial-Gerichte unter der Aufsicht des Kammergerichts, allein letzteres war keineswegs ausschließlich vom Kurfürsten abhängig. Nach der Kammergerichts-Ordnung vom Jahre 1516 wurden vielmehr von den 12 Mitgliedern des Kammergerichts nur vier vom Kurfürsten ernannt, sechs wurden von den Rittergutsbesitzern, zwei von den Prälaten und zwei von den Städten ernannt, so daß also zwei Drittel der Richter ihre Ernennung nicht dem Kurfürsten, sondern den Ständen zu danken hatten; übrigens waren sämmtliche Richter des Kammergerichts eidlich verpflichtet, nach den bestehenden Gesetzen zu entscheiden.

§. 2.

Die Rechte der Stände waren aber vorzugsweise geschützt durch die militairische Machtlosigkeit des Kurfürsten. Derselbe hatte bis zum dreißigjährigen Kriege gar kein stehendes Heer, wenn man nicht die 150 bis 200 Trabanten, welche er auch in Friedenszeiten hielt, als solches betrachten will. Im Fall eines Krieges hatte daher der Kurfürst bis zum dreißigjährigen Kriege nur die Wahl, entweder Söldner zu werben, — wozu er sich aber die Mittel von den Ständen bewilligen lassen mußte, da die Revenüen der Domainen und die sonstigen ordentlichen Einkünfte nur zu den Friedens-Ausgaben hinreichten, — oder die Ritterschaft und die streitbare Mannschaft der Städte aufzubieten. Dieses allgemeine Landesaufgebot bewies sich schon in der ersten Hälfte des dreißigjährigen Krieges als ganz unbrauchbar. Der Kurfürst war nicht im Stande, mit Hülfe der von ihm aufgebotenen Mannschaft den Durchmärschen und Verwüstungen der Truppen des Grafen v. Mansfeld, des Wallenstein und später der Schweden irgendwie Einhalt zu thun.

Aber auch schon im 16. Jahrhundert zeigte sich das allgemeine Landes-Aufgebot, obgleich es zu jener Zeit weit kriegstüchtiger war, als im 17. Jahrhundert, doch nur alsdann brauchbar, wenn die aufgebotenen Unterthanen mit dem Zwecke, zu welchem der Kurfürst sie aufrief, einverstanden waren.

Der beste Beweis hierfür ist der Kampf, in den der Kurfürst Joachim I. im Jahre 1528 mit einem Lausitzer Edelmann v. Minkwitz verwickelt war und über den Zimmermann in seiner Geschichte der Mark unter den Kurfürsten Joachim I. und II. und Pauly Band 2. Seite 541 seiner Geschichte des Preußischen Staates nähere Mittheilungen macht. Ein Herr von Minkwitz hatte im tiefsten Frieden mit einem Sächsischen Edelmann von Schlieben und 400 Reitern die Stadt Fürstenwalde in der Mark überfallen, um den dort befindlichen Bischof von Lebus gefangen zu nehmen, und hatte, da der Bischof entflohen war, die Stadt geplündert. Der Kurfürst erließ, um diesen Landfriedensbruch zu rächen, ein Aufgebot der streitbaren Mannschaft der Mark, allein das ganze Landesaufgebot, welches angeblich 40,000 Mann stark zusammenkam, zeigte sich so unbotmäßig, daß der Kurfürst es wieder nach Hause schickte und statt dessen einen Freibeuter, Namens Böhme, mit acht Mann absandte, um den v. Minkwitz zu überfallen und zu tödten. Als dieser Freibeuter bei Ausführung seines Auftrages entdeckt und getödtet war, gab der Kurfürst den Versuch auf, sich selbst gegen den v. Minkwitz Recht zu verschaffen und erlangte nur durch Vermittelung des Kaisers, daß der ꝛc. v. Minkwitz ihm eine Art Abbitte leistete.

Die Ursache, weshalb Kurfürst Joachim I. mit dem Landes-Aufgebot so gar Nichts ausrichten konnte, lag gewiß nicht im Mangel an Entschlossenheit Seitens Joachim des Ersten. Dieser hatte sich bei allen Gelegenheiten als ein äußerst energischer Regent bewiesen. Sie lag lediglich darin, daß in der Mark sowohl, als im übrigen Deutschland das Landesaufgebot überhaupt nur zu brauchen war, wenn Ritterschaft und Städte wollten. Auch der nachmalige Kurfürst Moritz von Sachsen, ein äußerst kriegerischer Fürst, ward z. B., als er gegen den Willen seiner Unterthanen im Jahre 1546 seinen Vetter den Kurfürsten Johann Friedrich von Sachsen mit Krieg überzogen hatte, von seinen Vasallen gänzlich in Stich gelassen.

Aehnlich wie in der Mark war die fürstliche Macht im 16. Jahrhundert auch in fast allen andern Staaten Deutschlands beschränkt, namentlich in den Territorien, durch deren Vereinigung der jetzige Preußische Staat gebildet ist. Nirgends hatten die Fürsten stehende Heere. An Ausübung unumschränkter fürstlicher Gewalt gegenüber den in allen Territorien bestehenden Ständen oder an eine dauernde Unterdrückung des Volks durch die Fürsten war daher nirgends zu denken.

Wir sehen dies recht klar bei der großen Bewegung Deutschlands zur Zeit der Reformation.

Im Erzbisthum Magdeburg z. B. ward von fast allen Städten die Reformation angenommen, meistens unter gewaltsamer Vertreibung eines Theils der Geistlichkeit, ohne daß der katholisch gebliebene Erzbischof dies hindern konnte. Auch in Pommern verbreitete sich die Reformation Anfangs ganz gegen den Willen der katholischen Landesherren. Diese mußten ruhig ansehen, wie in den meisten Städten die Reformation zum Theil gewaltsamer Weise eingeführt wurde, weil sie nicht die Mittel besaßen, es zu hindern. Ein Zeitgenosse, Sastrow, dessen Schilderungen höchst belehrend für die Zustände Deutschlands in jener Zeit sind, berichtet darüber (Theil I. Seite 43 der Lebensbeschreibung Sastrow's):

> „Zum andern kamen auch in's Land sonderlich in Hinterpommern etzliche Schwarmgeister — die reizeten ihre Zuhörer zum Bildestörmente, und lehrten auf der Kanzel, daß man die Fürsten mit Lumpen werfen und aus dem Lande jagen sollte .... die hatten im Lande einen trefflichen Anhang; der-

wegen die Fürsten gar still waren, und, da sie noch Papistischer Religion, um des großen Haufens willen still halten mußten.“

§. 3.

Wenn somit die ständische Verfassung, so wie solche bis zum dreißigjährigen Kriege in der Mark bestand, wohl geeignet war, die Unterthanen gegen Willkühr des Landesherrn zu schützen, so war dieselbe doch keinesweges dazu angethan, dem Lande eine Verwaltung und Rechtspflege zu sichern, welche den Anforderungen einer gebildeten Nation hätte entsprechen können.

Auch nachdem es dem Kurfürsten Joachim I. gelungen war, dem Faustrecht und der Wegelagerung der Edelleute ein Ende zu machen, also vom Anfang des 16. Jahrhunderts ab, sah es bis zur Regierung des großen Kurfürsten mit der öffentlichen Sicherheit in der Mark traurig aus. Als einen Beweis, wie vielfache Räubereien und gewaltsame Diebstähle vorkamen und wie schlecht dabei das Verfahren der Criminal-Gerichte war, wollen wir uns erinnern, daß z. B. unter dem strengen und kräftigen Joachim I. der Räuber Kohlhaas mit seiner Bande mehr als 10 Jahre lang Sachsen, Schlesien und die Mark plünderte, daß ferner nach dem Berichte gleichzeitiger Chronisten unter Joachim I. in einem Jahre von den Untergerichten wegen Begünstigung einer Räuberbande 100 Personen hingerichtet wurden, welche sämmtlich, wie sich hernach durch Entdeckung der wirklichen Verbrecher herausstellte, völlig unschuldig gewesen waren. Die grausame Härte der Criminalgerichte konnte dem Mangel einer guten Polizei nicht abhelfen. Diese Härte wird erklärlich, wenn wir einen Blick auf das materielle Strafrecht und auf das Strafverfahren jener Zeit werfen. Als materielles Strafrecht bestand die im Jahre 1532 erlassene peinliche Halsgerichts-Ordnung Carl's V., die sogenannte Carolina, welche bekanntlich keine anderen Strafen als die Todesstrafe, verstümmelnde und sonstige Leibesstrafen kannte und welcher die Gefängnißstrafe noch gänzlich unbekannt war.

Was das Verfahren in Straffachen betrifft, so bestand in der Mark wie im übrigen Deutschland zu jener Zeit neben dem Anklage-

Prozesse der Inquisitions-Prozeß, in welchem der Richter das Recht hatte, falls dringende Verdachtsgründe vorlagen, durch die Tortur das Geständniß des Angeklagten zu erzwingen. Die Gerichtsbarkeit über Edelleute und sonstige eximirte Personen stand dem Kammergericht zu, die über andere Personen den landesherrlichen Justiz-Aemtern, sowie den städtischen und Patrimonialgerichten, welche der Regel nach mit Personen, die nicht studirt hatten, besetzt waren. Es hatte ferner in Criminal-Prozessen bis zum Ende des 17. Jahrhunderts in der Mark der Angeklagte nicht das Recht der Appellation; es wurden vielmehr die von den Gerichten gefällten Criminal-Urtheile, sogar Todes-Urtheile, ohne Weiteres vollstreckt. Uns erscheint eine solche Praxis jetzt als fast unglaublich, denn es dünkt uns widersinnig, daß das Recht der Berufung auf einen höheren Richter, welches jedem Verklagten zusteht, der zur Zahlung weniger Thaler verurtheilt ist, einem zum Tode verurtheilten Menschen nicht zustehen soll. Ein Menschenleben, sollte man meinen, hätte doch höher geachtet werden müssen, als ein geringes Vermögens-Object; dennoch war die Appellation, wie Müller in seiner 1670 gedruckten practica Marchica, resolutio XXXIX. bezeugt, noch unter der Regierung des großen Kurfürsten zwar bei fiscalischen Untersuchungen, in denen auf Geldstrafe erkannt wurde, zugelassen, jedoch bei Untersuchungen wegen Todschlags, Giftmischerei, beim Hexenprozesse, bei Anklage des Raubes, der Meuterei u. s. w., kurz bei eigentlichen Criminal-Sachen unzulässig. Nur den schreiendsten Uebelständen ward durch Zulassung der Nullitätsklage gegen Erkenntnisse der Untergerichte abgeholfen. Auch in den andern deutschen Reichsländern war in dieser Zeit das Rechtsmittel der Appellation in Criminal-Sachen meistens ausgeschlossen. Das Reichskammergericht hatte allerdings Anfangs auch in Criminal-Sachen die Appellation zugelassen. Die Reichsstände hatten sich jedoch hierüber als eine dem bisherigen Herkommen zuwider laufende Neuerung beschwert und durch Beschluß des Reichstags von 1530 war ausdrücklich bestimmt, daß in Criminal-Sachen künftig keine Appellation an das Reichskammergericht stattfinden solle (siehe Müller's practica Marchica, resol. XXXIX.)

Eine rasche und prompte Handhabung der Justiz in Criminal-Sachen würde allerdings bei dem langsamen Verfahren des Reichskammergerichts und der meisten andern höhern Gerichte in Deutschland im 16. und 17. Jahrhundert ohne Ausschließung der Appellation kaum zu erreichen gewesen sein; allein die Raschheit und Wohlfeilheit des Criminal-Verfahrens jener Zeit ward leider oft genug auf Kosten der materiellen Gerechtigkeit erkauft. Um einen Begriff von der Art des Verfahrens zu geben, braucht man nur einmal actenmäßige Darstellungen von Criminal-Prozessen aus dem 16. und 17. Jahrhundert, wie solche z. B. Sastrow in seiner Lebensbeschreibung mehrfach giebt, namentlich aber Hexenprozeß-Acten gelesen zu haben. Die Hexenprozesse hatten allerdings ihren Hauptgrund in dem zum Theil noch aus den Zeiten des Heidenthums stammenden, in ganz Deutschland verbreiteten Aberglauben, ihre entsetzliche Verbreitung muß man jedoch wesentlich der schlechten Gerichtsverfassung, welche Deutschland im 16. und 17. Jahrhundert hatte, zuschreiben. Sie waren nämlich, obwohl die Möglichkeit der Zauberei im Alterthume wie im Mittelalter fast allgemein anerkannt war, doch in der Art, wie sie in Deutschland bis Ende des 17. Jahrhunderts stattfanden, sowohl dem Römischen als dem Kanonischen Rechte völlig unbekannt und im offenbaren Widerspruch mit dem Geiste des Römischen wie Kanonischen Rechts. Selbst der große Luther, der in dieser Beziehung leider die Vorurtheile seiner Zeit theilte, klagte darüber:

> „die gelehrten Juristen wollten in den Fällen, wo durch Besprechen Jemand einen andern beschädigt habe, keine Strafen erkennen.“

Es fehlt auch nicht an Beispielen, daß schon im 16. Jahrhundert die größtentheils aus gelehrten Juristen zusammengesetzten höhern Gerichte, namentlich das Reichskammergericht, in den Hexenprozessen die Rechte der Angeklagten zu schützen suchten, doch waren solche Versuche meistens fruchtlos, weil eben von den Untergerichten in Criminal-Sachen der Regel nach keine Appellation stattfand. Der Einfluß des Volksaberglaubens und der Praxis der Untergerichte war vielmehr so stark, daß im Laufe des 16. und 17. Jahrhunderts allmälig auch die Universitäten und Spruchcollegien die mit dem Römischen und Kanonischen Rechte in klarem Widerspruch stehende Praxis der Hexenprozesse anerkannten und billigten, bis endlich gegen Ende des 17. Jahrhunderts hauptsächlich durch den Einfluß des großen Thomasius die Ueberzeugung von der völligen Vernunftwidrigkeit dieser Prozesse die Oberhand gewann.

§. 4.

Fernere Nachtheile der ständischen Verfassung.

Die ständische Verfassung führte aber ferner auch zu ungerechter Bevorzugung der allein auf dem Landtage vertretenen Privilegirten gegenüber der Masse der Nation. Die Zwangs- und Bann-Rechte der Städte, die Stapelrechte, die Zunftprivilegien, welche sämmtlich Bevorzugungen der Städte vor dem flachen Lande enthalten, stammen alle aus der Zeit der ständischen Verfassung. Die Stellung der adlichen Rittergutsbesitzer gegenüber den freien Bauern sowohl als den Leibeigenen war ferner bei dieser ständischen Verfassung, da sowohl Gerichtsbarkeit als Polizei-Verwaltung ganz in den Händen der Edelleute war, eine solche, daß ein Mißbrauch derselben Seitens der Edelleute kaum zu verhüten war. Man hat oft die Behauptung aufgestellt, daß in der Zeit des Faustrechts und des Fehdewesens der Stand der freien Bauern gewaltsam durch den Adel unterdrückt und in den Zustand der Leibeigenschaft oder Gutsunterthänigkeit versetzt sei. Diese Behauptung halten wir für durchaus unrichtig. Die Leibeigenschaft hat zwar in der Mark, wie in den meisten andern Gegenden Deutschlands seit den ältesten Zeiten bestanden, allein niemals, so weit die Geschichte reicht, sind sämmtliche Bauern Leibeigene gewesen.

Es mögen unzweifelhaft einzelne Fälle der Unterdrückung und viele Fälle der Plünderung von Bauern in der Zeit des Faustrechts vorgekommen sein, allein eine generelle Unterdrückung des ganzen Standes ist in jener Zeit nicht denkbar, denn gerade in der Zeit des Faustrechts waren auch die freien Bauern wehrhaft und eben in Folge der allgemeinen Rechtsunsicherheit mit den Waffen vertraut und gewohnt, ihre Rechte selbst zu vertheidigen; sie würden daher den Versuch einer allgemeinen Unterdrückung gewiß mit entschlossenem Widerstande zurückgewiesen haben.

Ein Beispiel, wie ein einfacher Bürger noch im 16. Jahrhundert sich gegen ungerechte Unterdrückung auf gewaltsame Weise selbst Recht zu verschaffen suchte, giebt der bekannte Märkische Roßkamm Kohlhaas, der wegen des durch einen Sächsischen Edelmann erlittenen Unrechts nicht blos diesem Edelmann, sondern dem Kurfürsten von Sachsen selbst Fehde ansagte, und unter der Regierung Joachim I., wie bereits erwähnt, mehr als 10 Jahre lang ganz Sachsen, Schlesien und die Mark beunruhigte.

Weit gefährlicher als die Zeit des Faustrechts war für das Bestehen des freien Bauernstandes die Zeit von der zweiten Hälfte des 16. Jahrhunderts an bis zum dreißigjährigen Kriege, denn in dieser Zeit war mit der zunehmenden Gesittung das Fehderecht, aber auch die allgemeine Wehrhaftigkeit des Volks verschwunden, daher mochte bei den Edelleuten das Streben zunehmen, durch Mißbrauch ihrer gutsherrlichen Rechte auch die freien Bauern in den Zustand von Leibeigenen herabzudrücken. In Mecklenburg wurden vorzugsweise in dieser Zeit die Höfe der freien Bauern von den Rittergutsbesitzern eingezogen und zu ihren Gütern gelegt. Wenn wir dies und die strengen Verordnungen erwägen, welche noch der große Kurfürst, Friedrich Wilhelm I. und Friedrich II. zum Schutze der Bauern gegen die Bedrückungen der Gutsherren für nöthig hielten, obwohl die Verhältnisse schon seit der Regierung des großen Kurfürsten eine solche Unterdrückung weniger als früher begünstigten, so darf man kaum zweifeln, daß wenigstens seit der zweiten Hälfte des 16. Jahrhunderts bis zum dreißigjährigen Kriege die Rechte, welche die gutsherrliche Polizei-Gewalt, die Patrimonial-Gerichtsbarkeit und die ganze ständische Verfassung den Gutsherren gaben, auch in unserm Vaterlande vielfach zur Unterdrückung des Bauernstandes gemißbraucht sind.

§. 5.

Die alte ständische Verfassung ward nun in der Mark schon zur Zeit des dreißigjährigen Krieges durch den großen Kurfürsten materiell aufgehoben. Der Anstoß hierzu kam nicht von Innen, sondern von Außen. Bei den Stürmen des dreißigjährigen Krieges zeigte es sich, daß der Kurfürst, obwohl er außer der Mark bereits Ostpreußen und einen Theil von Jülich besaß, nicht die Macht hatte, das Land gegen die Verwüstungen der kriegführenden Mächte zu schützen. Als er z. B. im Jahre 1627 zum Schutze der Mark das Landvolk und die Ritterschaft, so wie die wehrhafte Bürgerschaft der Städte aufbieten wollte, zeigte sich das allgemeine Landesaufgebot als ganz unbrauchbar; der Kurfürst konnte nicht 3000 Mann Landvolk zusammenbringen, auch die Bürgerschaft der Städte verweigerte den Gehorsam; über die Bürgerschaft von Berlin berichtete z. B. der Kanzler Pruckmann an den Kurfürsten: „Der Herr omnes in Berlin sagen, sie wollten nicht auf die Wache ziehn, da sie nur Calvinisten bewachen sollten, die .... alle dem Teufel angehörten.“

Unter diesen Umständen versuchte es der Kurfürst eine Armee zu werben, allein die Stände bewilligten dazu nicht die nöthigen Geldmittel.

In Folge dessen konnte es nicht verhindert werden, daß nach mancherlei Durchzügen der kriegführenden Truppen gegen Ende des Jahres 1627 Wallenstein die ganze Mark besetzte und beinahe drei Jahre lang mit seiner Armee occupirt hielt. Um die für jene Zeiten sehr bedeutende Armee zu unterhalten, mußte das Land außerordentliche Steuern aufbringen. Die Neumark allein zahlte binnen drei Jahren über 1 Million Thaler baar. Um die Einquartirung und Verpflegung der Truppen zu regeln, den Vorspann zu beschaffen und die zum Unterhalt der Truppen nöthige Steuer zu erheben, wurde durch Rescript des Kurfürsten vom 16. April 1627 das Amt der Kreis-Commissarien eingeführt, die zwar von den Ständen der einzelnen Kreise erwählt, vom Kurfürsten jedoch als landesherrliche Beamten bestätigt wurden und später den Namen Landräthe erhielten.

So entstand während des dreißigjährigen Krieges das für die Verwaltung unseres Staats so wichtig gewordene Institut der Landräthe; die Bevölkerung der Mark überzeugte sich zugleich von der Nothwendigkeit, dem Kurfürsten dauernd die Mittel zum Unterhalt einer stehenden Armee zu bewilligen. Schon Kurfürst Georg Wilhelm schrieb daher, bald nach jener Occupation des Landes durch Wallenstein, ohne die Stände zu fragen, eine Contribution d. i. Grund- und Einkommen-Steuer aus, um Truppen anzuwerben und zu unterhalten; er erklärte dabei offen, „eine solche Ausschreibung von Steuern ohne Befragung der Stände sei nicht Herkommens, aber bei solchem extraordinairen Zustande vermöge er es nicht zu ändern und werde kein Unterthan, der Verstand hat und ohne Passion ist, sich darüber beschweren können.“ Als nun der große Kurfürst im Jahre 1640 zur Regierung kam, fand er eine allerdings wenig zahlreiche geworbene Armee vor, so wie eine seit 1625 unter dem Namen Contribution dauernd bestehende Grundsteuer; er verstärkte sofort seine Armee, führte bessere Disciplin bei derselben ein, und es gelang ihm, schon während der letzten Jahre des dreißigjährigen Krieges sein Land vor ferneren Verwüstungen zu schützen.

Behufs des Unterhalts der Armee mußte er die Contribution forterheben, jedoch ward in den Städten bereits 1641 statt derselben die Accise eingeführt, weil diese leichter zu erheben war.

Auch nach dem Westphälischen Frieden behielt der Kurfürst die stehende Armee unter den Waffen und fuhr fort, die einmal eingeführten Abgaben zu erheben. Das Land hatte sich an diese Abgaben seit mehr als 20 Jahre gewöhnt. Die Stände der Mark waren durch die Drangsale des langen Krieges hinlänglich belehrt, wie nothwendig die Bewilligung der Geldmittel zum Unterhalt eines stehenden Heeres für die Sicherheit des Vaterlandes sei, auch würden sie kaum noch die Macht gehabt haben, dem Kurfürsten die geforderten Abgaben zu verweigern; sie bewilligten auf dem 1653 geschlossenen Landtage die Forterhebung der einmal eingeführten Steuern. Die Macht der Märkischen Stände war seit jener Zeit thatsächlich aufgehoben. Sie traten zwar noch wiederholt zusammen, um dem Kurfürsten Bitten vorzutragen, und figurirten bei feierlichen Huldigungen, aber einen wesentlichen Einfluß auf die Politik des Landes haben sie nicht wieder geübt.

§. 6.

Die Landstände der Herzogthümer Pommern und Magdeburg, sowie der kleinern Territorien, als Halberstadt, Minden u. s. w., konnten noch weniger als die Märkischen Stände es wagen, dem großen Kurfürsten die von ihm erforderten, für jene Zeit sehr bedeutenden Abgaben zu verweigern.

Nur bei den Ständen des Herzogthums Preußen fand der große Kurfürst einen erheblichen Widerstand in Bezug auf die von ihm gestellten Forderungen. Diese Stände hatten bis Mitte des siebenzehnten Jahrhunderts nicht geringere verfassungsmäßige Rechte, als die Stände der Mark bis zum dreißigjährigen Kriege gehabt hatten. Der König von Polen als Oberlehnsherr des Herzogthums Preußen wachte mit Sorgfalt über Aufrechthaltung dieser ständischen Rechte; der Adel des Herzogthums Preußen, welcher vielfach mit dem Polnischen Adel verwandt war, hatte ein unverkennbares Streben nach derselben Machtvollkommenheit und Ungebundenheit, welche der Polnische Adel bereits erlangt hatte.

Als nun im Jahre 1655 Krieg zwischen Polen und Schweden ausbrach, ward auch Preußen in diesen Krieg verwickelt; der große Kurfürst konnte, da die Preußischen Stände keine genügenden Geldmittel zur Werbung von Truppen bewilligten, zum Schutze des Herzogthums Preußen außer wenigen Truppen, welche er aus der Mark herbeizog, nur das allgemeine Landesaufgebot verwenden, welches letztere sich bei dieser Gelegenheit als völlig unbrauchbar bewies. Die Folge war, daß Preußen auf's Furchtbarste verheert wurde. Namentlich drangen im October 1656 Kosacken und Tartaren als Bundesgenossen der Krone Polen in Preußen ein, brannten 13 Städte und eine große Anzahl Dörfer und Flecken nieder, mordeten 23000 Menschen und schleppten 34000 als Sclaven fort. (v. Orlich, Geschichte des großen Kurfürsten Thl. I. S. 279.) Und als nach dieser furchtbaren Heimsuchung, welche den Nachtheil der völligen Wehrlosigkeit des Landes so klar dargelegt hatte, der Kurfürst von den Ständen Geldmittel forderte, um zum Schutze des Landes Truppen unterhalten zu können, waren die Stände im Jahre 1657 nur mit der größten Mühe zu bewegen, die Geldmittel zum Unterhalt von 5000 Mann Truppen zu bewilligen, verlangten aber zugleich mit vielem Nachdrucke, der Kurfürst möge die Juden und Mennoniten, welchen er im Lande Schutz gewährt hatte, aus Preußen ausweisen! (v. Orlich, Thl. I. S. 280 ff.)

Durch den Frieden von Oliva im Jahre 1660 wurde die Lehnsherrlichkeit der Krone Polen über Preußen aufgehoben; die Stände von Preußen waren hiermit keineswegs einverstanden: sie weigerten sich Anfangs, dem Kurfürsten als nunmehr souveränem Landesherrn von Preußen zu huldigen. Erst nachdem derselbe die Rechte der Stände neu bestätigt und ihnen ausdrücklich das Recht eingeräumt hatte, daß Streitigkeiten zwischen ihm und den Ständen durch ein Schiedsgericht von 13 Personen sollten entschieden werden, von denen er und die Stände je 6 ernennen sollten und welche dann eine dreizehnte Person als Obmann zu wählen hätten, erst da erlangte der Kurfürst im Jahre 1663 die Huldigung der Preußischen Stände. (v. Orlich, Thl. I. S. 333.)

Er behielt nun die Abgaben, welche im Jahre 1657 während des Schwedisch-Polnischen Krieges eingeführt waren, nach dem Frieden von Oliva bei. Sie gaben ihm die Mittel zum Unterhalt eines stehenden Heeres. Allerdings fehlte es auch nach der Huldigung vom Jahre 1663 nicht an Streitigkeiten zwischen ihm und den Preußischen Ständen. Es war wohl vorzugsweise der Macht, welche der Kurfürst durch seine Armee besaß, zu verdanken, daß derselbe bei diesen Streitigkeiten immer seinen Willen durchsetzte, ohne daß es je zu einer Entscheidung des im Jahre 1662 mit den Ständen vereinbarten Schiedsgerichts gekommen wäre. Allerdings griff der Kurfürst dabei zuweilen zu Mitteln, die sich vom Standpunkte des Rechtes aus nicht vertheidigen lassen; wir wollen hier nur an die widerrechtliche Verhaftung des Herrn v. Kalkstein in Warschau im Jahre 1670 und dessen demnächst auf Befehl des Kurfürsten erfolgte Hinrichtung erinnern; allein es läßt sich nicht verkennen, daß der Kurfürst, wenn er nicht sein Land zur Beute mächtiger Nachbarn werden lassen wollte, wie solches hundert Jahre später mit Polen der Fall war, gezwungen war, die Macht der Stände zu brechen und durch eine starke, wohldisciplinirte Armee, zu deren Unterhalt er hoher Steuern nicht entbehren konnte, sich gegenüber fremden Mächten eine Achtung gebietende Stellung zu verschaffen. Bei den Preußischen Ständen fand der Kurfürst bei diesem Streben durchaus keine Unterstützung. Noch im Jahre 1678 während des Kriegs mit den Schweden verlangten dieselben unter andern auf's Nachdrücklichste:

> „daß der Stände Unterthanen, Knechte und Dienstboten auf dem Lande und in den Städten wegzuwerben nicht gestattet werde,"

sie wollten also, während ihre Vorfahren den Kriegsdienst unter den Fahnen des Landesherrn als erste Lehnspflicht angesehen hatten, selbst während des Krieges nicht einmal ihren Unterthanen gestatten, ohne ihre Erlaubniß in den Dienst des Landesherrn einzutreten! Gegenüber ihren Unterthanen wollten die Preußischen Edelleute damals die Herren spielen, ohne den Kurfürsten als Herrn über sich zu erkennen und ohne dem Wohle des Vaterlandes Opfer bringen zu wollen. Von der Stimmung der Bauern und Gutsunterthanen ist bei dem Streit zwischen dem Kurfürsten und den Ständen gar nicht die Rede. Es scheint nicht, daß sie große Sympathie für die Rechte der Stände gehabt haben. Als der Streit des Kurfürsten mit den Ständen im Jahre 1662 kurze Zeit hindurch zu einem offenen Kampfe zu führen schien, ging der Erstere eine Zeitlang mit dem Gedanken um, die in Preußen bestehende Leibeigenschaft, deren Entstehung er für eine widerrechtliche erklärte, aufzuheben. Er gab jedoch diesem Plane, der vielleicht nur darauf berechnet war, die Stände einzuschüchtern, weiter keine Folge.

§. 7.

Am Schluß der Regierung des großen Kurfürsten war die landesherrliche Macht im ganzen Brandenburg-Preußischen Staate so fest begründet, daß die Rechte der Stände in sämmtlichen Territorien fast nur noch nominelle waren. Unter den folgenden Regierungen ward Seitens der Stände kein Versuch gemacht, die verlornen Rechte wieder zu gewinnen. Wenn sich zuweilen in der einen oder andern Provinz der Versuch einer Opposition der Stände gegen den Landesherrn zeigte, ward doch jeder solche Versuch ohne großen Kampf vereitelt.

Als z. B. im Jahre 1717 der Landtags-Marschall der Provinz Preußen gegen Einführung der allgemeinen Grundsteuer protestirte, wies Friedrich Wilhelm I. diesen Protest ohne Weiteres zurück mit der berühmten Aeußerung: „Ich stabilire die Souveraineté wie einen Rocher von Bronce,“ und führte demnächst im Jahre 1719 die allgemeine Grundsteuer unter dem Namen des General-Hufen-Schosses ohne Zustimmung der Stände ein. Noch bezeichnender für die Art und Weise, in der Friedrich Wilhelm I. die ständischen Rechte auffaßte, ist die Anweisung, welche er dem General-Directorio am 20. December 1722 ertheilte, als die Stände des Herzogthums Magdeburg gegen die Abgabe der Ritterpferde-Gelder protestirten, und in welcher es wörtlich heißt: „Wir sind doch Herr und König und können thun, was wir wollen.“

Zwar erfolgte keine formelle ausdrückliche Aufhebung der alten ständischen Rechte, vielmehr hatten sowohl Friedrich Wilhelm I. unterm 11. September 1714 als Friedrich II. im Jahr 1740 diese Rechte vor der Huldigung ausdrücklich gewährleistet, allein materiell wurden diese Rechte weder in der Mark Brandenburg noch im Herzogthum Preußen oder einem andern Landestheile weiter erheblich beachtet.

Auch in den Landestheilen, welche seit dem Tode des großen Kurfürsten zur Monarchie hinzukamen, wurden überall die Rechte der Stände materiell aufgehoben, so namentlich durch Friedrich II. in Schlesien; nur in Ostfriesland und Neufchatel behielten die Stände bei der Huldigung ihre hergebrachten Rechte, ohne daß das Beispiel dieser beiden Landestheile den Rest der Monarchie zur Nachfolge gereizt hätte. Zur gänzlichen Machtlosigkeit der Stände trug ohne Zweifel wesentlich der Umstand bei, daß seit dem Tode des großen Kurfürsten die stehende Armee, welche unbedingt zur Verfügung des Landesherrn stand, fortwährend vermehrt war, und daß in Folge dessen, wegen der zum Unterhalt der Armee durchaus nothwendigen

Ausgaben, auch der Betrag der jährlichen Steuern hatte bedeutend erhöhet werden müssen. Das starke stehende Heer verschlang die besten Kräfte des Landes, allein seit der Zeit des dreißigjährigen Krieges war der Staat durch die äußeren Verhältnisse gezwungen gewesen, dasselbe zu unterhalten. Der große Kurfürst hatte während der Jahre 1656—1660 sich an dem Kriege zwischen Schweden und Polen betheiligen müssen, von 1672—1679 war er mit Frankreich und Schweden in Krieg verwickelt gewesen, von 1683—1699 hatte der Krieg des deutschen Reichs mit den Türken, von 1688—1696 auch der gegen Frankreich und demnächst wieder von 1700—1714 der Spanische Erbfolgekrieg gedauert, an welchen Kriegen sämmtlich der Brandenburg-Preußische Staat Theil genommen hatte. Fast ohne Ausnahme waren diese Kriege für den Preußischen Staat unvermeidlich gewesen, indem sie theils zum Schutze der Preußischen Monarchie selbst, theils zum Schutze des deutschen Reichs in Folge der dem Kurfürsten als Reichsstand obliegenden Verpflichtungen geführt waren.

Bei diesen Verhältnissen konnten die Stände vom Tode des großen Kurfürsten an bis zur Regierung Friedrich Wilhelm's I. nicht wagen, dem Landesherrn die zum Unterhalt der Armee nothwendigen Geldmittel zu verweigern und es fehlte ihnen daher auch an der reellen Macht, um einen ernstlichen Versuch zur Wiedererringung ihrer zur Zeit des großen Kurfürsten verlornen Rechte zu machen.

Was nun aber die Regierungen Friedrich Wilhelm's I. und Friedrich's II. betraf, so war bei der kräftigen Persönlichkeit dieser Herrscher an ein Geltendmachen früherer ständischer Rechte natürlich nicht zu denken. Auch war unter Friedrich Wilhelm I. die Macht des Landesherrn auch in pecuniärer Beziehung schon so gestiegen, daß der Fürst Leopold von Dessau dem Könige alles Ernstes den Vorschlag machen konnte, er möge alle Rittergüter ankaufen und sich so zum ganz unbeschränkten Gebieter und einzigen Gutsherrn in seinem Lande machen, welchen Vorschlag der König glücklicher Weise nach reiflicher Ueberlegung nur auf Rath des Generals v. Grumbkow ablehnte.

§. 8.

Was die Verwaltung des Landes betraf, so blieb in der ganzen Zeit bis 1806 die Polizei-Gewalt in den Städten in den Händen der Magistrate, auf dem Lande in den Händen der Rittergutsbesitzer und auf den Domänen in denen der Gutspächter. Die Schulzen der Dörfer wurden von den Gutsbesitzern oder Domänen-Pächtern ernannt und verpflichtet und waren von denselben in jeder Beziehung abhängig. Die Polizei-Verwaltung der Rittergutsbesitzer und Domänen-Pächter ward zunächst beaufsichtigt durch die Landräthe, welche jedoch nicht, wie gegenwärtig, königliche und besoldete Beamte waren, sondern von den Rittergutsbesitzern jedes Kreises aus ihrer Mitte gewählt und vom Könige nur bestätigt wurden. Auch pflegten sie und zwar wenigstens viermal im Jahre die Rittergutsbesitzer und Abgeordneten der im Kreise befindlichen Städte zu einem Kreistage behufs Berathung der Interessen des Kreises zu berufen. Ueber den Landräthen als Provinzial-Verwaltungs-Behörden standen die seit dem Mittelalter bestehenden Amtskammern, welche vorzugsweise die Erhebung der Domänen-Gefälle und der Steuern für die Civil-Verwaltung zu besorgen hatten, und die seit der Zeit des großen Kurfürsten bestehenden Kriegs-Commissariate, welche die zum Unterhalt des Militairs erforderlichen Steuern zu erheben, außerdem die Servis- und Aushebungs-Sachen zu besorgen hatten. Beide Behörden wurden von Friedrich Wilhelm I. durch Patent vom 24. Januar 1723 zu Kriegs- und Domänen-Kammern vereinigt, welche sämmtliche Polizei-, Domänen-, Forst-, Steuer- und Militair-Sachen in den Provinzen zu verwalten hatten und somit in ihrer Bedeutung im Ganzen unseren heutigen Regierungen entsprechen. Sie übten auch die Gerichtsbarkeit aus über solche Sachen und Gegenstände, welche mit der Finanz-Verwaltung und Landespolizei unmittelbar in Verbindung standen.

Sie standen sämmtlich unter dem in Berlin befindlichen General-Ober-Finanz-Kriegs- und Domänen-Directorium, gewöhnlich genannt General-Directorium. Dieses war im Jahre 1723 gleichzeitig mit der Vereinigung der Amtskammern und Kriegs-Commissariate durch Friedrich Wilhelm I. mittelst Vereinigung des bis dahin bestandenen General-Commissariats und des früher Geheime Hof-Kammer genannten General-Finanz-Directorii gebildet worden.

Was die Städte betrifft, so hatte schon Friedrich Wilhelm I. dieselben namentlich in Bezug auf ihre Finanz-Verwaltung einer sehr genauen Aufsicht unterworfen, welche durch besondere Steuer-Räthe unter Aufsicht der Kriegs- und Domänen-Kammern geführt wurde. Diese Bevormundung wurde unter Friedrich II. schon im Jahre 1740 in der Art vermehrt, daß die Magistrate der Städte eigentlich gar keine Ausgaben ohne Genehmigung der ihnen vorgesetzten Staats-Behörden machen konnten.

§. 9.

Die höchste berathende und verwaltende Behörde, welche dem Landesherrn zur Seite stand, war in der ganzen Zeit bis 1806 der Staatsrath. Derselbe war bereits im Jahre 1604 vom Kurfürst Joachim Friedrich gestiftet und hatte bei seiner Gründung aus 9 Mitgliedern bestanden. Er hatte ursprünglich als höchste Verwaltungs-Behörde collegialisch häufig unter persönlichem Vorsitz des Landesherrn über die vom letztern ihm zugewiesenen äußern und innern Landes-Angelegenheiten berathen. Die Zahl seiner Mitglieder wechselte vielfach. Unter Friedrich II. bestand er aus den sämmtlichen Staats-Ministern und denjenigen Hofbeamten, welche Minister-Rang hatten. Es wurde zu jener Zeit neben dem Namen Staatsrath der Name Geheimes Staats-Ministerium üblich. Es war noch unter Friedrich II. Vorschrift, daß alle Mitglieder des Staatsraths protestantischer Religion sein mußten, und wurde daher der Graf Schafgotsch, obwohl er als Oberstallmeister von Amtswegen Mitglied des Staatsraths hätte sein müssen, nicht in denselben eingeführt. (Preuß, Geschichte Friedrich's II., Bd. IV. S. 462). Seine Bedeutung hatte aber schon damals wesentlich abgenommen durch Einrichtung des bereits erwähnten General-Directorii und durch die unter Friedrich Wilhelm I. erfolgte Bildung des sogenannten Cabinets-Ministerii oder Departements für die auswärtigen Angelegenheiten, welches letztere die auswärtigen Angelegenheiten selbstständig zu bearbeiten hatte. Noch mehr hatte der Staatsrath an Bedeutung dadurch verloren, daß seit Friedrich Wilhelm I. die Regenten an den Sitzungen desselben fast gar nicht theilnahmen, sondern auf schriftliche Berichte der Minister durch Befehle aus dem Cabinet entschieden.

§. 10.

Gerichts-Verfassung und Gerichts-Verfahren.

Was die Gerichts-Verfassung und das Gerichts-Verfahren betraf, so fand der große Kurfürst bei seinem Regierungs-Antritt einen in hohem Grade mangelhaften Zustand vor. Im Jahre 1646 schenkte er dem Kammergericht auf Veranlassung eines speciellen Falls, in welchem er Parteilichkeit des Gerichtshofes vermuthete, ein Gemälde, welches darstellte, wie König Kambyses von Persien einen Richter zur Strafe der Bestechung lebendig schinden ließ. Gewiß eine furchtbare Mahnung für den Gerichtshof, der ein solches Geschenk erhielt und ein trauriges Zeichen der Zeit, daß das Kammergericht nach dem Urtheile des Landesherrn einer solchen Mahnung bedurfte!

Die Mitwirkung der Stände bei Wahl der Kammergerichts-Räthe fiel mit dem Aufhören der regelmäßigen Stände-Versammlungen in der Mark von selbst hinweg, doch blieb noch bis in das 18. Jahrhundert hinein der Unterschied einer gelehrten und einer adlichen Bank der Mitglieder des Kammergerichts. Die Besetzung der übrigen, namentlich der Patrimonial- und städtischen Gerichte, blieb noch lange Zeit ganz die frühere. Noch unter der Regierung Friedrich Wilhelm's I. war die Mehrzahl der Untergerichte, namentlich der Patrimonial-Gerichte, nicht mit studirten Juristen besetzt. Nur für die Obergerichte schrieb die Kammergerichts-Ordnung vom 1. Mai 1709 vor, daß sämmtliche Mitglieder Rechtsgelehrte sein sollten. Die gleiche Anordnung für die Untergerichte erfolgt erst unter der Regierung Friedrich's II. durch den 1748 publicirten codex Fridericianus Theil III. Tit 4. §. 2—4.

Die Nachtheile der mangelhaften Besetzung der Untergerichte hatten sich bis zur Regierung Friedrich Wilhelm's I. hauptsächlich in der Criminal-Justiz gezeigt. Bis zu jener Zeit hatten die Untergerichte, sogar die Patrimonial-Gerichte der Regel nach Gerichtsbarkeit über Leben und Tod und fand gegen ihre Urtheile der Regel nach keine Appellation und überhaupt, wie die bereits §. 3 angeführte concl. 39 aus Müller's practica Marchica ergiebt, mit Ausnahme der gewiß selten zu begründenden Nullitätsklage, kein Rechtsmittel statt. Selbst die Vollstreckung der Todesstrafe erfolgte meistens ohne vorgängige Confirmation des Urtheils durch den Landesherrn. Es mochte ein Fortschritt gegen früher sein, daß die Untergerichte in der zweiten Hälfte des 17. Jahrhunderts anfingen der Regel nach auf schwere Strafen nicht selbst zu erkennen, sondern, wie schon die Carolina anrieth, die Acten zur Abfassung eines Erkenntnisses an Universitäten oder Schöppenstühle zu versenden; jedoch hatte diese Maßregel den sehr bedeutenden Nachtheil, daß in der Regel ein Richter erkannte, der weder den Angeklagten, noch die Zeugen sah, der Nichts vor sich hatte, als die oft so äußerst dürftigen Acten. Um sich einen Begriff von der strafbaren Leichtfertigkeit, Härte und Rechtsunkenntniß zu machen, mit der so häufig in Criminal-Sachen von den Gerichten verfahren wurde, braucht man nur manche von den landesherrlichen Verordnungen aus dem Ende des 17. und Anfang des 18. Jahrhunderts zu lesen. In der Magdeburger Polizei-Ordnung von 1688 heißt es z. B. Cap. 62. §. 1.:

> „Die Erfahrung bezeugt, wie bis anhero viele Urtheile in unserm Herzogthume Magdeburg zur Execution gebracht, da die Gefangenen mit keiner Defension gehört worden: damit nun auch hierunter die Gebühr beobachtet werden möge, als sollen alle und jede, welche die Ober- und Halsgerichte haben oder dieselben verwalten, ohne vorher geführte Defension kein Urtheil zur Execution bringen, es betreffe Landes-Verweisung, Stellung am Pranger, oder Leibes- und Lebensstrafe, sondern es soll der Gefangene vorher befragt werden, ob er mit seiner Defension nothdürftig gehört sein wolle ꝛc.“

In Cap. 60 §. 7 derselben Polizei-Ordnung heißt es ferner:

> „Und weil die Erfahrung giebt, daß öfters unsere Beamte und andere Gerichts-Obrigkeiten oder deren Gerichts-Ver-

walter ohne Noth die Gefangenen sofort in tiefe Straf-Gefängnisse werfen lassen, darinnen sie das Tageslicht nicht anschauen oder sich aufrichten und herumgehen können, welche Qual ihnen öfters so schwer als der Tod selbst ankommt ꝛc.“

Die Reform-Maßregeln Friedrich Wilhelm's I. und Friedrich's II. im Gebiete des Criminal-Prozesses und Criminalrechts sind nun so bedeutend, daß wir sie im Zusammenhange betrachten wollen.

§. 11.

Eine der ersten Verordnungen Friedrich Wilhelm's I., nämlich die Verordnung vom 13. December 1714, hob den Hexenprozeß gänzlich auf. Die Verordnung sagt: „nachdem der König glaubwürdig berichtet sei, daß bei den Hexen-Prozessen nicht allemal mit der gehörigen Behutsamkeit verfahren, sondern auf ungewisse Anzeigungen hin mancher unschuldiger Weise auf die Tortur, auch wohl um Leib und Leben gebracht sei, so solle der Prozeß in Hexen-Sachen untersucht und soviel möglich verbessert werden. Bis diese Verbesserung des Hexenprozesses erfolgen werde, solle kein auf Tortur oder gar auf Todesstrafe lautendes Urtheil gegen eine Hexe durch irgend ein Gericht vollstreckt werden, bevor solches vom Könige ausdrücklich confirmirt sei.

Die noch vorhandenen Brandpfähle, woran Hexen gebrannt sein, sollten weggenommen werden.“

In Folge dieser Verordnung hörten die Hexenprozesse in Preußen gänzlich auf, während im übrigen Deutschland noch lange einzelne derartige Prozesse zur Schmach der Gerichte vorkamen. Es wurde z. B. in Würzburg noch im Jahre 1749 eine 70jährige Nonne als Hexe verbrannt, in Landshut im Jahre 1756 ein armes dreizehnjähriges Mädchen als Hexe geköpft, ja noch 1782 in Glarus in der Schweiz eine Magd als Hexe hingerichtet! (Preuß, Friedrich II. Thl. III. Seite 211.)

Wenn die Verordnung vom 13. December 1714 ein Verfahren beseitigte, welches nur zu lange zur Schande der Justiz unseres Vaterlandes gedient hatte, so war für das ganze Criminal-Verfahren von höchster Wichtigkeit die von Friedrich Wilhelm I. am 6. Juli

1717 publicirte Criminal-Ordnung, die Anfangs blos für die Kurmark gegeben, bald auch in den übrigen Landestheilen eingeführt ward.

Diese Criminal-Ordnung schrieb vor, daß in allen Fällen die urtheilende Behörde eine andere als die Untersuchung führende sein sollte, und daß dem Angeklagten statt der Appellation das Rechtsmittel der weitern Vertheidigung zustehen solle. Im Uebrigen ward der damalige gemeinrechtliche Inquisitions-Prozeß, welcher wesentlich auf der Anwendung der Tortur beruhte, beibehalten. Friedrich Wilhelm I. erklärte jedoch bei allen schwereren Criminalstrafen namentlich der Todesstrafe die Einsendung der Acten an ihn zur Bestätigung vor Vollstreckung des Erkenntnisses für erforderlich.

Dies war eine Maaßregel von höchster Wichtigkeit, die im Wesentlichen bis auf die neueste Zeit in Geltung geblieben ist.

Zwar ward unter Friedrich II. bereits im Juni 1743 der Antrag gestellt, Behufs Ersparung von Kosten und Beschleunigung der Strafvollstreckung die Einsendung der Criminal-Erkenntnisse an den König mehr einzuschränken, allein der König wies diesen Antrag mit den Worten zurück:

> „Nein! Sie sollen alle Criminal-Urtheile einschicken, sonst würden dabei allerhand Inconvenienzien und daß die Leute in den Provinzen nach Gefallen gehudelt würden, entstehen können."

In der That hat nichts so außerordentlich wohlthätig auf die Praxis der Preußischen Gerichte in Criminal-Sachen eingewirkt, als gerade die stäte und sorgsame Einwirkung des Landesherrn, welche durch die Nothwendigkeit der landesherrlichen Bestätigung aller auf höhere Freiheitsstrafen oder Tod lautende Urtheile herbeigeführt ward.

§. 12.

Gerade die große Theilnahme, welche Friedrich Wilhelm I. der Ausübung der Criminal-Justiz schenkte, hatte aber auch die Folge, daß der König sich gewissermaßen als ersten Criminal-Richter des Landes ansah und demgemäß sich das Recht zuschrieb, Straf-Erkenntnisse der Gerichte nach seinem Ermessen nicht nur zu ermäßigen, sondern auch zu verschärfen. Zahlreiche Beispiele von rechtskräftigen Straf-Erkenntnissen, die Friedrich Wilhelm I. zum Nachtheile der Verurtheilten abänderte, liefert Förster in seiner Geschichte Friedrich Wilhelm's I. Thl. I. Seite 323 und Thl. II. Seite 269.

Das hervorragendste dieser Beispiele ist die Hinrichtung des Kriegs- und Domänen-Raths von Schlubuth zu Königsberg. Der rc. v. Schlubuth hatte bedeutende Summen, welche ihm amtlich anvertraut waren, unterschlagen. Das Criminal-Collegium in Berlin, an welches diese Sache zum Spruch überwiesen war, erkannte auf mehrjährige Festungsstrafe, indem es als Milderungs-Grund den Umstand berücksichtigte, daß Schlubuth hinreichende Caution gestellt habe, um den Ausfall zu decken. Der König bestätigte das Erkenntniß nicht. Als er hiernächst im Jahre 1731 nach Königsberg kam, ließ er den rc. v. Schlubuth sich vorführen, hielt ihm sein Vergehen vor und kündigte ihm an, daß er eigentlich den Galgen verdient habe. Der rc. v. Schlubuth erwiderte trotzig, es sei nicht Manier, einen Preußischen Edelmann aufhängen zu lassen, zumal er die vergriffenen Gelder wieder herbeischaffen werde. Der König gab darauf die kurze Antwort: „Ich will Dein schelmisches Geld nicht haben," ließ sofort auf dem Schloßplatze, dem Sessions-Zimmer der Kriegs- und Domänen-Kammer gegenüber, einen hohen Galgen errichten und wenige Tage darauf den von Schlubuth an diesem Galgen aufhängen vor den Augen des Königs und der Mitglieder der Kriegs- und Domänen-Kammer, die auf Befehl des Königs im Sessions-Zimmer versammelt waren.

So entsetzlich uns derartige Acte des Despotismus erscheinen müssen, so dürfen wir doch nicht übersehen, daß viele und angesehene Deutsche Rechtslehrer im vorigen Jahrhundert dem Landesherrn unbedingt das Recht der Straffschärfung zusprachen, wie z. B. aus Quistorp's Beiträgen zur Erläuterung von Rechtsmaterien Band I. Stück 3 Seite 93 hervorgeht, daß jedenfalls der König wirklich in dem Glauben stand, es sei sein Recht und seine Pflicht, die ergehenden Straf-Erkenntnisse nach seinem Ermessen zu mildern oder zu verschärfen, daß er auch Straffschärfung fast nur in solchen Fällen eintreten ließ, in denen er annahm, daß aus Rücksicht für den Rang und Stand des Angeklagten zu gelinde erkannt sei.

In Civil-Justiz-Sachen erlaubte sich der König ähnliche Einmischungen niemals. Die Civil-Prozesse, welche Fiscus gegen Privat-Personen führte, gingen, wie noch jetzt der Regel nach, meistens für den Fiscus verloren. So ungehalten der König hierüber auch oft war, griff er doch in derartigen Fällen niemals in den Lauf Rechtens ein, und als ihm einstens Seitens eines Kriegsraths gerathen ward, er solle doch den Geheimen Justizrath besser für das Königliche Interesse stimmen, schrieb der König zur Verfügung an den Rand:

„Narr, Narr, Narr, wenn Du nicht eines Obersten Sohn wärest, würde ich Dir hundert Prügel geben lassen.“

Das Recht der Schärfung der erkannten gerichtlichen Strafen hat übrigens noch Friedrich II. mehrfach ausgeübt.

§. 13.

Was das materielle Strafrecht betrifft, so bildete sich die Praxis mehr und mehr dahin aus, daß Gefängnißstrafen an Stelle der in der Carolina vorgeschriebenen verstümmelnden und Leibes-Strafen traten. Die eigentliche Gesetzgebung war im Gebiete des materiellen Criminalrechts nur wenig thätig. Bekannt ist eine Verordnung von 1735 über Hausdiebstahl, Kraft welcher jeder Hausbediente, der seinem Herrn über 3 Thlr. stehlen würde, an einem Galgen vor der Thüre des Bestohlenen aufgehenkt werden sollte. Diese Verordnung wurde in zwei Fällen gegen einen Bedienten und eine Köchin wirklich zur Anwendung gebracht und ward dann verdienter Maaßen nicht weiter beachtet.

Auch von einem andern noch grausameren Edict des Königs, die Zigeuner betreffend, darf man wohl annehmen, daß es nur in wenigen Fällen oder gar nicht zur Anwendung gekommen ist. Bereits am 24. November 1710 hatte Friedrich I. befohlen, alle Zigeuner (Männer und Weiber, jung und alt) aufzuhenken. Am 4. Januar 1726 schrieb nun Friedrich Wilhelm I. vor, die Zigeuner, welche das 16. Jahre erreicht hätten, sollten gehenkt, die jüngern aber in Zuchthäuser gebracht werden.

§. 14.

Im Ganzen erfreute sich der Preußische Staat unter Friedrich Wilhelm I. einer innern Ruhe und Rechts-Sicherheit, wie wenige Theile Deutschlands damals sich deren rühmen konnten und wie solche auch unter der kräftigen Regierung des großen Kurfürsten nicht stattgefunden hatte.

Bis zum Anfang des 18. Jahrhunderts war selbst in der Umgegend von Berlin offener Straßenraub etwas Alltägliches gewesen. Wie es in Süd-Deutschland mit der öffentlichen Sicherheit stand, zeigen die Geschichten der organisirten Würtembergschen und Baierschen Räuberbanden, die unter einem Hannickel, dem Baierschen Hiesel u. s. w. bis in die achtziger Jahre des vorigen Jahrhunderts bestanden, und aus deren Resten sich noch im Anfang unseres Jahrhunderts die Bande des Schinderhannes bildete. Auch in Schlesien hatte es bis zur Preußischen Besitznahme im Jahre 1740 mit der öffentlichen Sicherheit höchst traurig ausgesehen. Es war, wie der bekannte Jurist Klein in seiner Selbstbiographie mittheilt, (Preuß, Thl. I. S. 200) ganz gewöhnlich gewesen, daß die Orts-Obrigkeiten mit den in ihrem Gebiete hausenden Räuberbanden im Einverständniß standen. Vor den Thoren von Breslau z. B. trieb bis 1740 eine Räuberbande unter einem gewissen Mandube ihr Wesen; die Mitglieder der Patricier-Familien von Breslau erzählten es nun, wie Klein mittheilt, mit Wohlgefallen, wie der Räuberhauptmann Mandube sie bei später Zurückkunft von einer Spazierfahrt als Schutzwache gegen seine Raubgenossen bis an das Thor begleitet und sich sodann ehrerbietig von ihnen beurlaubt habe, für welche Gefälligkeit der Magistrat natürlich durch schmähliche Nachsicht dem Räuber seinen Dank abstattete. Wenn nun ähnliche Zustände in Preußen unerhört waren, so hatte man dies vorzugsweise zwei Umständen zu verdanken, nämlich einmal der strengen Aufsicht, welcher sämmtliche Behörden von oben her unterworfen waren, und sodann der für jene Zeit vorzüglichen Ordnung des Armenwesens, welche durch Friedrich I.

und Friedrich Wilhelm I. eingeführt wurde und von Epoche machender Wichtigkeit für die öffentliche Sicherheit unseres Vaterlandes geworden ist.

Wir müssen diese Gesetze über Armenpflege näher betrachten.

§. 15.

Die Armenpflege war während der ersten Hälfte des Mittelalters in den Händen der christlichen Kirche gewesen und war in den meisten Ländern des westlichen Europa's die Vorschrift des Kanonischen Rechtes in Geltung, daß ein Viertel des Zehnten zur Armenpflege zu verwenden sei. Die geordnete kirchliche Armenpflege hatte jedoch schon vor der Reformation aufgehört und war dadurch eine weltliche Armenpflege nothwendig geworden. Diese fiel, soweit sie nicht in den Händen milder Stiftungen war, überall in Deutschland den Gemeinden zu, stand also in unserm Vaterlande auf dem Lande, sowie die übrige Gemeinde-Verwaltung überall unter Aufsicht der adlichen Gutsbesitzer oder der Domänen-Pächter. Der Staat kümmerte sich bis Ende des 17. Jahrhunderts nur insofern um die Armenpflege, als er die Gemeinden anwies, wie es in der Verordnung vom 18. November 1684 (Mylius Corpus Constit. Magdeburgicarum P. I. S. 93) wörtlich heißt: „soviel immer möglich,“ für ihre Armen zu sorgen. Wenn nun die Gemeinden es nicht möglich fanden, genügend für ihre Armen zu sorgen, so blieb es den letztern überlassen, sich selbst durch Betteln oder Stehlen vor dem Hungertode zu schützen und sie pflegten dann auch schaarenweise bettelnd durch das Land zu ziehen.

Es war in dieser Beziehung in unserm Vaterlande nicht anders als überhaupt in Deutschland.

Ueber das in dieser Beziehung in Deutschland im Anfang des 18. Jahrhunderts geltende Recht giebt am besten Aufschluß Leyser in seinem meditt. ad Pandectar. specimen 324. (Volumen V. Seite 318 ff.)

Er selbst ist zwar der Meinung, daß es die Pflicht jedes Landesherrn sei, dafür zu sorgen, daß die wirklich Hülfsbedürftigen unter seinen Unterthanen nicht Hungers stürben, allein er gründet diese Ansicht nicht auf ein positives Gesetz, sondern blos auf das Gebot der christlichen Menschenliebe und führt an, daß nicht nur die Praxis in den verschiedenen Staaten Deutschlands eine sehr verschiedene, sondern daß auch die Theorie keinesweges einig sei, indem viele Rechtsgelehrte namentlich auch Hugo Grotius der Meinung seien, der Landesherr habe keine Verpflichtung, für die Unterstützung der Armen zu sorgen, er könne vielmehr diese Unterstützung der freien Mildthätigkeit der Privaten überlassen, auf die Gefahr hin, daß, wenn diese Mildthätigkeit nicht ausreiche, die Armen Hungers stürben.

§. 16.

In Preußen ward nun durch die Verordnung vom 10. Februar 1715 (Rabe, Band I. Abth. I. S. 406) für die ganze Monarchie vorgeschrieben, daß das Betteln für die Zukunft hart bestraft werden solle, jede „Stadt und Dorf aber ihre Armen nothdürftig versorgen" solle.

Um die Ausführung dieses Edicts zu sichern, ward den Obrigkeiten, welche wirklich hülfsbedürftige Arme durch Verweigerung der Unterstützung zwingen würden zu betteln, eine Geldstrafe angedroht und wurden die Fiscäle, welche eine ähnliche Stellung hatten wie unsere jetzigen Staatsanwälte, angewiesen, aufs Strengste gegen die in Bezug auf die Armenpflege nachlässigen obrigkeitlichen Personen einzuschreiten. Den Pastoren ward es ferner zur Pflicht gemacht, sich solcher Armen, die nicht gehörig unterstützt würden, anzunehmen und sollten die Pastoren auf dem Lande allmonatlich über den Zustand der Armen in ihren Gemeinden an die vorgesetzte geistliche Behörde berichten. Um die nöthigen Geldmittel zur Armenpflege zu erlangen, sollten in den Gemeinden Collecten gehalten werden. Die Beisteuer zu diesen Collecten war keine blos freiwillige, es war vielmehr verordnet, daß die „Morosi, welche sich zu ihrer christlichen Schuldigkeit in Bezug auf die Beiträge zur Collecte gar nicht anschicken wollten," durch ihre Geistlichen ermahnt, und falls sie sich an die Ermahnung nicht kehren würden, durch den Magistratus loci genöthigt werden sollten, ein Gewisses nach Proportion ihrer

Nahrung und ihres Vermögens zu zahlen. In Bezug auf die Armen-Cassen erfolgten noch speciellere Vorschriften durch die allgemeine Verordnung vom 21. Juni 1725 (Rabe, Band I. S. 728), namentlich ward durch diese Verordnung bestimmt, daß in allen Fällen, wo eine Gemeinde nicht im Stande sei, genügend für ihre Armen zu sorgen, dem Könige selbst wegen der erforderlichen Remedur Anzeige geschehen solle. Eine stete Beaufsichtigung der Armenpflege der Gemeinden durch vorgesetzte Beamte namentlich durch die Steuer-Räthe ward angeordnet und vorgeschrieben, daß kräftige Bettler nöthigenfalls durch Strafen zur Arbeit angehalten werden sollten.

Dies ist der wesentliche Inhalt der Gesetze vom 10. Februar 1715 und 21. Juni 1725, welche in ihren Hauptgrundzügen mit den Anordnungen übereinstimmen, welche bereits unter dem Vater Friedrich Wilhelm's I., König Friedrich dem Ersten, durch die Verordnungen vom 10. April 1696, 19. November 1698, 1. Juni 1699, 18. März 1701 und 19. September 1708 (Mylius C. Constitt. Magdeb. P. I. S. 117 ff.) theils für einzelne Landestheile, theils für den ganzen Staat vorgeschrieben waren.

Diese Verordnungen hatten nun nicht blos den Erfolg, daß der unverschuldeten Armuth mehr als früher abgeholfen wurde, sondern auch, daß das Herumstreifen von Bettler-Horden, welche, wie in jenen Gesetzen wiederholt geklagt wird, oft Schaarenweise unter Drohungen bettelten, häufig auch Diebstahl, Raub, Brandstiftung, Mord und Erpressung verübten, allmälig fast ganz aufhörte.

Dies war von der weitgreifendsten Wirkung für die öffentliche Sicherheit und die Criminalrechtspflege. So lange der Staat es fast ganz dem guten Willen der einzelnen Gemeinden überlassen hatte, ob sie ihre Armen verpflegen wollten oder nicht, hatte man den Armen, welche von ihren Ortsbehörden Nichts erhielten, nicht verwehren können, bettelnd im Lande umherzuziehen. Der umherziehende Bettler wurde aber oft durch Noth getrieben zum Diebe oder Räuber, auch gesellten sich, wie in jenen Verordnungen vom 10. April 1696 rc. wiederholt erwähnt wird, gewerbsmäßige Räuber zu den umherziehenden Bettlerschaaren; nur durch eiserne Strenge gegen Diebe und Räuber hatte daher während des 16. und 17. Jahrhunderts einigermaßen die öffentliche Sicherheit aufrecht erhalten werden können.

Als nun aber in Folge der besseren Armenpflege es möglich geworden war, das Betteln und namentlich das bettelnde Umherziehen im Lande zu verbieten, fiel die Hauptpflanzschule der Verbrecher hinweg, die Zahl der offenen Raub-Anfälle verringerte sich und es konnten die Strafen, namentlich in Bezug auf Raub und Diebstahl, allmälig ohne Nachtheil für die öffentliche Sicherheit ermäßigt werden.

Die Gesetze über Armenpflege stehen daher mit der Criminalrechtspflege und dem Zustande der öffentlichen Sicherheit im allerengsten Zusammenhange, daher dürften die unter Friedrich I. und Friedrich Wilhelm I. gegebenen Gesetze über Armenpflege, sowie betreffend das Verbot des Bettelns, in ihren Wirkungen für die öffentliche Sicherheit kaum geringer zu schätzen sein, als die Maaßregeln, welche Kurfürst Joachim I. im Anfang des 16. Jahrhunderts Behufs Unterdrückung der Wegelagerung der Gutsbesitzer ergriffen hatte.

§. 17.

Wir wollen hier zunächst eine Uebersicht der Reformen anknüpfen, welche unter Friedrich dem II. in Bezug auf das Verfahren in Criminal-Sachen und das Criminal-Recht selbst in's Leben traten. Schon unmittelbar nach seiner Thronbesteigung durch Cabinets-Ordre vom 3. Juni 1740 schaffte Friedrich II. den Gebrauch der Folter „außer bei dem crimen laesae Majestatis und Landesverrätherei und denen große Mordthaten oder wo viele Delinquenten.... implicirt sind" gänzlich ab. Auch für die in dieser Verordnung noch ausgenommenen Fälle ward demnächst die Tortur durch verschiedene Verordnungen aus dem Jahre 1754 und 1756 in allen Theilen der Monarchie beseitigt.

Es war diese Aufhebung der Tortur eine der edelsten und schönsten Regenten-Handlungen Friedrich's II.

Preußen ging in dieser Beziehung sämmtlichen Staaten des Continents von Europa mit seinem Beispiele voran. Nur langsam folgten die übrigen Staaten diesem Beispiele nach. In Kur-Sachsen ward die Folter erst im Jahre 1770, in Frankreich erst durch die Edicte vom 24. August 1780 und vom November 1789, in manchen Staaten Deutschlands erst zu Anfang des 19. Jahrhunderts aufgehoben.

Die Abschaffung der Tortur hatte die Folge, daß in solchen Fällen, in welchen wegen des vorhandenen Verdachts bis dahin auf Tortur erkannt und, je nachdem der Angeklagte in Folge derselben zum Geständniß gebracht wurde oder nicht, die Verurtheilung oder Freisprechung erfolgt war, nunmehr auf eine sogenannte außerordentliche Strafe erkannt wurde, welche nur wenig geringer war, als die ordentliche Strafe.

Was die Competenz der Gerichte betrifft, so ward dieselbe allmälig dahin regulirt, daß alle Urtheile, welche auf mehr als zweijährige Freiheitsstrafe lauteten, vor der Publication dem Justiz-Minister zur Bestätigung eingesandt werden mußten. (Hymmen's Beiträge Bd. 4. S. 218, Bd. 6. S. 225). Bis zu dieser Bestätigung galten die Erkenntnisse blos als Gutachten; sobald sie vom Justiz-Minister bestätigt waren, stand dem Angeklagten das Rechtsmittel der weitern Vertheidigung zu; Todesstrafen und Freiheitsstrafen von mehr als 10 Jahren konnten nur nach Bestätigung des Erkenntnisses durch den König vollstreckt werden. (S. 41, 42 von Theil II. Ergänz. der Preußischen Rechtsbücher von Gräff, Koch &c.)

Die neuere Zeit hat die Nothwendigkeit der ministeriellen Bestätigung der Erkenntnisse, welche zu dem mündlichen Gerichtsverfahren nicht paßte, mit Recht beseitigt; für die Verhältnisse des vorigen Jahrhunderts ist sie aber gewiß wohl geeignet gewesen. Ueberhaupt aber steht die große Sorgfalt, welche seit Friedrich Wilhelm I. Seitens der Centralbehörden unseres Staates und der Landesherren selbst der Verwaltung der Criminal-Justiz gewidmet ward, im schärfsten Contraste mit den von uns geschilderten Zuständen des Criminal-Verfahrens im 16. und 17. Jahrhundert und bildet einen schönen Beweis des Fortschritts unseres Vaterlandes in wahrer Humanität und zugleich der Thätigkeit unserer Könige.

§. 18.

Auch was das materielle Strafrecht betrifft, waren die Reformen Friedrich's II. höchst bedeutend.

Es hatte bis zu jener Zeit auf Grund der Carolina die Strafe des Säckens der Kindesmörderinnen bestanden, und war dieselbe in der Anwendung noch dadurch verschärft worden, daß man die Kindesmörderinnen zwang, selbst den ledernen Sack zu nähen, in dem sie ersäuft wurden. Diese Strafe verwandelte der König durch Cabinets-Ordre vom 31. Juli 1740 in die Strafe der Hinrichtung durch das Schwert. Auf eine Milderung der Strafe des Diebstahls wirkte namentlich hin die Cabinets-Ordre vom 8. April 1750 (Hymmen's Beiträge, 4. Sammlung, S. 172). In dieser Ordre verschärft der König zunächst für einen speciellen Fall die wegen Raubes erkannte zweijährige Festungsstrafe auf zehnjährige Festungsstrafe, — ein Beweis, daß auch Friedrich II. nicht minder, wie sein Vater, sich zu einer derartigen Strafschärfung für berechtigt und verpflichtet hielt, — und bemerkte sodann, „es sei seine Intention, daß bei Diebstählen, welche aus Unbesonnenheit, Armuth und dergleichen Umständen mehr, begangen worden, nicht die Todesstrafe oder eine sehr lange und harte Festungsstrafe erkannt werden solle; in den Fällen aber, wo der Dieb einen Mord begangen oder bei Straßenräubereien oder gewaltthätigem Einbrechen und darauf geschehenem Binden der Leute oder wenn ganze Diebes-Complotts sich finden, solle den Umständen nach die Todesstrafe oder doch die Strafe der Festungsarbeit auf Zeitlebens oder doch auf eine vieljährige Zeit erkannt werden.“

Der König selbst spricht in einem Briefe an Voltaire vom 8. October 1777 seine Ansichten über das Criminal-Recht folgendermaßen aus, indem er uns zugleich über die Zahl der damaligen Todesurtheile interessante Aufschlüsse giebt:

> „Die Carolina ist mir bekannt. Ich habe diese alten Gesetzbücher durchblättert, als ich es nöthig fand, den Völkern an der Küste des Baltischen Meeres bessere Gesetze zu geben. Diese waren, wie man von den Drakonischen zu sagen pflegte,

mit Blut geschrieben. In dem Verhältnisse, wie die Völker civilisirter werden, muß man auch die Gesetze mildern. Wir haben es gethan und befinden uns wohl dabei.... Um Ihnen einen deutlichen Begriff davon zu geben, muß ich Sie mit unserer Bevölkerung bekannt machen. Diese beläuft sich nur auf 5,200,000 Seelen.... Seitdem nun unsere Gesetze gemildert worden sind, werden bei uns im Durchschnitt jährlich nur 14, höchstens 15 Todesurtheile gefällt. Das kann ich Ihnen um so zuverlässiger sagen, da ohne meine Unterschrift Niemand zur Festungsstrafe verurtheilt und ebenso Niemand hingerichtet werden darf, wenn ich die Sentenz nicht bestätigt habe. Die meisten Delinquenten sind Kindesmörderinnen. Andere Mordthaten giebt es wenig und noch seltener ist Straßenraub.“

Gewiß nicht ohne Grund äußerte der König gegen den Minister von Zedlitz einmal seine Freude darüber, „daß in Preußen unter allen Europäischen Staaten die wenigsten Hinrichtungen nöthig befunden würden.“ (Preuß, Friedrich der Große, Theil 3. S. 377).

In dem Verhältniß, daß auf 5,200,000 Einwohner im Jahre 1777 14 bis 15 Hinrichtungen jährlich vorkamen, müßten jetzt (1860) auf 17 bis 18 Millionen Einwohner 40 bis 50 Hinrichtungen jährlich kommen; glücklicher Weise ist diese Zahl jetzt beträchtlich geringer, was seinen Grund theils darin, daß die Zahl der Verbrechen abgenommen hat, theils und hauptsächlich wohl in der Milderung der gesetzlichen Strafen haben mag. Was namentlich das Verbrechen des Kindesmords betrifft, so fing man bekanntlich aus sehr triftigen Gründen in den letzten Jahrzehnden des vorigen Jahrhunderts an, für den Fall, daß die Tödtung des Kindes unmittelbar bei oder nach der Geburt erfolgt, statt der Todesstrafe eine längere Freiheitsstrafe zur Anwendung zu bringen und hat seitdem die Zahl der Hinrichtungen wegen Kindesmords, über deren Häufigkeit Friedrich II. klagte, erheblich abgenommen.

§. 19.

Was das Justiz-Wesen im Allgemeinen betrifft, so ist noch zu erwähnen, daß bereits Friedrich Wilhelm I. im Jahre 1737 den Freiherrn von Cocceji zum Ministre Chef de Justice ernannte und dadurch zuerst ein einheitliches Justiz-Ministerium in dem Sinne, welchen wir jetzt mit dieser Behörde verbinden, in's Leben gerufen hatte. Neben dem Ministre Chef de Justice behielten übrigens noch drei andere Staatsbeamten als Präsidenten der obersten Gerichtshöfe den Titel Justiz-Minister bei. Höchst wichtig waren nun die Aenderungen sowohl der Justiz-Verfassung als des Civil-Prozeß-Verfahrens, welche unter der Regierung Friedrich's II. in's Leben traten. Es fand unter dieser Regierung eine doppelte Reform des Civil-Prozeß-Verfahrens und der Gerichts-Verfassung statt, zuerst unter Leitung des Justiz-Ministers Cocceji im Jahre 1748 und sodann unter Leitung von Carmer und Suarez im Jahre 1781. Beide Reformen wurden mit derjenigen schonungslosen Energie durchgeführt, welche fast alle Regierungs-Handlungen Friedrich's II. auszeichnet. Schon bei der Cocceji'schen Justiz-Reform wurden z. B. die Mitglieder der Landes-Justiz-Collegien fast aller Provinzen entlassen und nur diejenigen, welche für brauchbar und unbescholten erachtet wurden, — was keineswegs bei allen der Fall gewesen zu sein scheint, — wieder angestellt. Dieses harte Verfahren läßt sich nur dadurch erklären, daß in der That der Richterstand zu jener Zeit auch in den Landes-Justiz-Collegien viele unfähige oder verderbte Mitglieder zählte. In Magdeburg z. B. hatte es, wie Dietz in seinem Archiv Magdeburgischer Rechte berichtet, vor der Cocceji-schen Justiz-Reform für völlig unmöglich gegolten, in einem Prozesse gegen ein Mitglied des Landes-Justiz-Collegii Recht zu erhalten.

Abgesehen von der Aenderung der Personen in Bezug auf die Besetzung der Richterstellen führte die Cocceji'sche Justiz-Reform zu einer am 4. April 1748 unter dem Namen eines codex Fridericianus Marchicus publicirten Prozeß-Ordnung. Sie ward dem Namen nach nur als Entwurf publicirt, weil die Stände noch mit ihrem Gutachten über sie gehört werden sollten, doch erhielt sie vorbehaltlich der nachträglichen Revision der Stände, welche nie erfolgt ist, sofort Gesetzeskraft.

Die wesentlichen Neuerungen dieser Justiz-Reform bestanden in folgenden drei Punkten:

1) Es ward dem Richter nicht mehr gestattet, die Acten zur Abschaffung des Erkenntnisses an eine Universität zu übersenden, vielmehr wurden die Gerichte genöthigt, alle vor sie gebrachten Prozesse selbst zu entscheiden.

2) Auch hinsichtlich der Untergerichte ward vorgeschrieben, daß sie nur mit rechtskundigen Personen zu besetzen seien, woraus von selbst folgte, daß den Königlichen Justiz-Behörden das Recht der Prüfung und Approbation der anzustellenden städtischen und Patrimonialrichter zufiel.

Die Nothwendigkeit der Anstellung rechtskundiger Richter auch bei den Untergerichten war durch das Verbot der Acten-Versendung herbeigeführt. Der Grund, weshalb nicht schon früher eine bessere Besetzung der Untergerichte erfolgt war, war wohl hauptsächlich der, daß es im 17. und noch im Anfang des 18. Jahrhunderts an einer genügenden Zahl rechtskundiger Bewerber um Untergerichts-Stellen gefehlt hatte.

Die Zahl der Studirenden war bekanntlich in jener Zeit lange nicht so groß wie jetzt, unter denen aber, die studirten, überwogen an Zahl bei Weitem die Theologen; die Zahl derer, die sich dem Studio der Rechte widmeten, war bis zum Anfange des 18. Jahrhunderts in Deutschland verhältnißmäßig sehr klein gewesen.

3) Es ward durch die Cocceji'sche Reform für den ganzen Staat, jedoch mit Ausschluß der Provinz Preußen, ein höchster Gerichtshof in Berlin constituirt. Die Bedeutung dieses Gerichtshofs stieg noch dadurch, daß in Folge des unbeschränkten privilegii de non appellando, welches der Kaiser im Jahre 1751 ertheilte, die Gerichtsbarkeit des Reichskammergerichts für den ganzen Staat vollständig hinwegfiel. In den Jahren 1772 und 1774 ward die Competenz des höchsten Gerichtshofs auch auf die Provinz Preußen ausgedehnt und ward demselben officiell zuerst 1772 der Namen des Geheimen Ober-Tribunals beigelegt, welcher bekanntlich erst durch

die Verordnung vom 2. Januar 1849 in den Namen des Ober-Tribunals verwandelt ist.

Das Civil-Prozeß-Verfahren selbst blieb bei der Cocceji'schen Justiz-Reform im Wesentlichen das alte, übereinstimmend mit den Vorschriften des gemeinen Deutschen Civil-Prozesses, wie sich solcher aus den Bestimmungen des Römischen und Kanonischen Rechts und der Reichsgesetze allmälig gebildet hatte.

§. 20.

Weitgreifender noch war die durch Carmer und Suarez im Jahre 1781 bewirkte Justiz-Reform. Der äußere Anlaß zu derselben ist bekannt.

Friedrich II. war seit Jahren mit den Gerichten und deren Verfahren in Civilprozessen höchst unzufrieden gewesen. Bei Gelegenheit der Klage eines Müllers Arnold gegen einen Landrath von Gersdorf im Jahre 1779 glaubte er, offenbar mit Unrecht, daß das Kammergericht aus Rücksicht für den Rang des Verklagten den Arnold mit seiner Klage abgewiesen habe. Er cassirte daher eigenmächtig die Richter, welche bei Entscheidung des Prozesses lediglich ihrer Ueberzeugung gefolgt waren, verschaffte durch einen Machtspruch dem Arnold wieder den Besitz seiner Mühle, zwang die Richter, dem Arnold noch eine bedeutende Entschädigung zu zahlen und ließ sie überdies ohne Urtheil und Recht mit Festungsstrafe belegen. Außerdem aber entließ er den damaligen Justiz-Minister Großkanzler von Fürst und schenkte nun den Reform-Vorschlägen des neuen Großkanzlers von Carmer, welche er selbst früher verworfen hatte, Gehör.

Das durch Carmer eingeführte neue Prozeß-Verfahren beruhte auf einem Principe, welches bis dahin in keiner ältern oder neuern Gesetzgebung angenommen war, nämlich darauf, daß der Richter im Civilprozesse die Wahrheit durch persönliches Befragen der Parteien von Amtswegen ermitteln und demgemäß seine Entscheidung fällen sollte. Es war somit das Untersuchungs-Verfahren aus dem Criminal-Prozeß in den Civil-Prozeß übertragen.

Folge dieses Princips war, daß der Advocaten-Stand gänzlich

aufgehoben ward und die Parteien gezwungen wurden, bei allen Prozessen persönlich vor Gericht zu erscheinen. Sämmtliche Advocaten wurden daher, soweit sie nicht anderweite Anstellungen erhielten, durch die Verordnung von 1781 brodlos gemacht. Sehr bald zeigte es sich aber, daß das neue Princip sich nicht vollständig durchführen ließ. Schon im Jahre 1783 führte man die Advocaten unter dem Namen von Justiz-Commissarien wieder ein, behielt indessen die Verpflichtung des Richters, die Wahrheit im Civil-Prozeß von Amtswegen zu ermitteln, sowie die Verpflichtung der Parteien zum persönlichen Erscheinen vor Gericht bei, und wurden die Bestimmungen der Verordnung von 1781 mit dieser im Jahre 1783 getroffenen Modification in die 1795 publicirte Allgemeine Gerichts-Ordnung aufgenommen.

Nachdem durch die Verordnungen vom 1. Juni 1833 und 21. Juli 1846 die Principien der Justiz-Reform vom Jahre 1781 im Wesentlichen beseitigt sind, ist man wohl darüber einig, daß die Anwendung des Untersuchungs-Verfahrens auf den Civil-Prozeß durchaus verwerflich ist und somit die Justiz-Reform von 1781 als eine verfehlte zu betrachten ist, doch darf man nicht verkennen, daß das Verfahren auf Grund jener Verordnung wenigstens in den ersten Jahrzehnden seiner Anwendung sich im ganzen gut bewährt und den Beifall der öffentlichen Meinung erworben hat.

Der Grund hierfür war wohl der, weil in jener Zeit der Advocaten-Stand nicht die gleiche Ehrenhaftigkeit und Tüchtigkeit hatte, wie der Richter-Stand. Gegenwärtig freilich darf unser Anwalt-Stand sich gewiß in jeder Beziehung dem Richter-Stande an die Seite stellen; ist es ja doch dahin gekommen, daß, so oft eine Anwalts-Stelle in einem größern Orte vacant wird, sich ältere Richter und Gerichts-Directoren oft zu Dutzenden um dieselbe bewerben, daß überhaupt der größere Theil unserer jüngern Juristen die Anstellung als Richter nur als eine Durchgangsstellung betrachtet, um zu Anwalts-Stellen zu gelangen.

§. 21.

Die processualische Reform des Jahres 1781 gab Anlaß, daß

Friedrich II. ein Project, welches er bereits im Jahre 1746 gehabt hatte, wieder aufnahm, indem er den Großkanzler von Carmer beauftragte, für die ganze Monarchie ein allgemeines Deutsches Gesetzbuch auf Grund des bestehenden positiven Rechts und des Naturrechts ausarbeiten zu lassen. Diesem Auftrag genügte von Carmer, hauptsächlich unterstützt von dem unermüdlich thätigen Suarez, durch Abfassung des Allgemeinen Land-Rechts, welches jedoch erst unter der Regierung Friedrich Wilhelm's II. vollendet ward und im Jahre 1794 Gesetzeskraft erhielt.

Ehe wir jedoch näher auf den Inhalt desselben eingehen, wird es nöthig sein, einen Blick auf die Aenderungen im Gebiete des materiellen Rechts zu werfen, welche seit der Regierung des großen Kurfürsten stattgefunden hatten.

§. 22.

Während die ständischen Rechte des Adels und der Städte schon durch den großen Kurfürsten beseitigt wurden, blieben alle dem Privatrecht angehörigen Vorrechte des Adels und der Städte bestehen. Betrachten wir einzelne dieser Vorrechte näher!

Bis zur Zeit des großen Kurfürsten hatte der Adel in den einzelnen Landestheilen das Recht, daß Niemand ein Rittergut erwerben konnte, der nicht zum angesessenen Adel gehörte oder mit dessen Genehmigung das Indigenat erlangte.

Noch der aus Oestreich eingewanderte Feldmarschall Dörflinger mußte, um in Pommern Rittergüter besitzen zu können, das Pommersche Indigenat sich von den dortigen Ständen ertheilen lassen. An Bürgerliche wurde dies Indigenat wohl nur höchst selten ertheilt.

So lange der Adel als solcher die wichtigsten ständischen Rechte besaß, dabei die Verwaltung des Landes im Wesentlichen in Händen hatte und zugleich eine wenig controllirte Gerichtsbarkeit und Polizei-Gewalt über seine Gutsunterthanen ausübte, war es natürlich, daß nicht jedermann ohne Unterschied zum Erwerb eines adlichen Guts und damit zugleich zum Eintritt in alle ständischen Rechte zugelassen werden konnte, und daß die Stände über diese Zulassung entschieden. Durch Aufhebung der alten landständischen Verfassungen fiel eigentlich der Hauptgrund für die Beschränkungen des Erwerbs der Rittergüter hinweg, allein der Adel glaubte zu seiner Erhaltung das ausschließliche Recht des Besitzes der Rittergüter nicht entbehren zu können. Man behielt daher die alte Beschränkung bei, nur mit der Modification, daß jeder Preußische Edelmann in jeder Provinz Rittergüter erwerben konnte und daß an die Stelle der Ertheilung des Indigenats durch die Stände der Provinz, wenn es sich um Erwerb eines Rittergutes durch einen Bürgerlichen handelte, die Genehmigung des Landesherrn trat, welche indessen nur höchst selten ertheilt wurde.

Die Gutsherrliche Polizei-Gewalt, das Patronatrecht und die Patrimonial-Gerichtsbarkeit, letztere freilich, wie unsere vorstehende Ausführung ergiebt, immer mehr beschränkt und controllirt durch die Aufsicht der landesherrlichen Gerichte, blieben bestehen.

Neu eingeführt ward das dem gemeinen Deutschen Recht unbekannte Verbot der Ehe zwischen Edelleuten und Frauenzimmern aus dem Bauer- oder niedern Bürgerstande, gleichsam als hätte man absichtlich die Trennung der Stände verschärfen wollen. Das Verbot findet sich zuerst in der Magdeburger Polizei-Ordnung Cap. VI. §. 7. und ward durch das Edict vom 8. Mai 1739 (C. Const. Marchicarum Contin. I. S. 251) für den ganzen Staat eingeführt, mit der Maßgabe, daß eine derartige Ehe den Verlust des Adels zur Folge haben sollte.

Was die Zunft- und Gewerbsprivilegien der Städte betrifft, so hatte der große Kurfürst bereits im Jahre 1668 die Absicht, dieselben sämmtlich aufzuheben; doch führte er diese Absicht, wegen des heftigen Widerspruchs, den er fand, nur in wenigen von ihm neu gegründeten Städten aus. (von Orlich, Geschichte des Preußischen Staates im 17. Jahrhundert, Thl. I. S. 451). Im Ganzen blieben auch unter den demnächst folgenden Regierungen die Zunft- und Gewerbsprivilegien der Städte unverändert bestehen.

§. 23.

Was die gutsherrlich-bäuerlichen Verhältnisse betrifft, so war es eine Haupttendenz der Gesetzgebung zu verhüten, daß die Gutsbesitzer nicht ihre obrigkeitliche Gewalt zum Einziehen der Bauergüter mißbrauchen sollten. Schon im Jahre 1670 beschwerte sich der große Kurfürst darüber, daß der Märkische Adel so vielfach Bauergüter einziehe. Fast unter jeder der folgenden Regierungen ergingen dann auch Verordnungen, welche das Einziehen von Bauergütern durch Edelleute bei namhafter Geldstrafe verboten und anordneten, daß jede wüst werdende Bauernstelle sofort mit einem Hofwirth besetzt werde. Derartige Verordnungen sind unter andern am 14. März 1739 von Friedrich Wilhelm I., ferner von Friedrich II. am 17. Juni und am 12. August 1749, ferner am 11. August 1762 erlassen (Bd. 7. S. 123 der Korn'schen Edicten-Sammlung).

Daß diese Verordnungen zum Schutze des Bauernstandes nöthig waren, ist ein Beweis der gedrückten Lage dieses Standes in jener Zeit; jedenfalls haben dieselben aber es verhindert, daß nicht die Bauerhöfe allmälig fast ganz durch die Rittergutsbesitzer aufgekauft und eingezogen sind, wie solches in Mecklenburg und Neu-Vorpommern im 17. und 18. Jahrhundert geschehen ist.

Als einen Beweis, wie sehr wenigstens in manchen Districten die Gutsunterthanen des Schutzes bedurften, müssen wir noch das Patent Friedrich's I. vom 3. August 1709 (Mylius, C. C. March. T. 4. Abth. 2. Cap. 3. Nr. 11.) und das sogenannte Prügel-Mandat Friedrich Wilhelm's I. von 1738 betrachten. Schon in ersterer ist verboten, daß „hinfüro kein Beamter, Hof- oder Jagdbedienter, er sei wer er wolle, bei Vermeidung harter Bestrafung, sich unterstehn solle, die Unterthanen ferner zu schlagen oder zu prügeln, sondern wenn selbige excediren, sollen sie mit Gefängniß oder auf andere Weise nach vorhergegangener Untersuchung der Sache abgestraft werden."

Das Prügel-Mandat vom 4. April 1738 (Dr. Förster, Friedrich Wilhelm I. Thl. II. S. 274) ist gerichtet gegen „das barbarische Wesen, die Unterthanen gottloser Weise mit Prügeln oder Peitschen wie das Vieh anzutreiben," es verbietet ernstlich „künftig die Unterthanen auf den Domainen mit Prügeln zur Arbeit anzutreiben" und gestattet nur, daß, „falls die Unterthanen nicht recht arbeiten, solche in den Stock gespannt oder ihnen der Spanische Mantel umgehängt, auch auf den Fall, daß dies bei den einen oder andern nicht verfangen will; solche auf einige Zeit mit Festungs-Arbeit bestraft werden. Was die Preußischen Lande (Ostpreußen) betrifft, so wollen Se. Majestät solche hierunter ausgenommen und dieses Verbot dahin nicht extendirt haben, weil das Volk daselbst sehr faul, gottlos und ungehorsam ist."

§. 24.

Dies Mandat sollte in den Krügen angeschlagen und daselbst den Unterthanen vorgelesen werden. Was die Leibeigenschaft betrifft, welcher in der zweiten Hälfte des 17. Jahrhunderts ein sehr großer Theil des Bauernstandes unterworfen war, so ward dieselbe durch eine Anzahl Verordnungen in allen Provinzen allmälig in das Verhältniß der Unterthänigkeit verwandelt. Dies geschah bereits in Ostpreußen durch eine Verordnung Friedrich Wilhelm's I. vom Jahre 1717, in einem Theile von Pommern durch die Verordnung vom 22. März 1719, für ganz Pommern in der Bauer-Ordnung von 1764 und endlich für Ost- und West-Preußen durch Verordnung vom 8. November 1773. Für den ganzen Staat erging noch während des siebenjährigen Krieges das Circular vom 7. Juni 1761, betreffend die verbotene Verhinderung der Heirathen der Unterthanen. Schon gegen Ende der Regierung Friedrich's II. war daher im Wesentlichen der Zustand hergestellt, den das Allgemeine Landrecht in Theil II. Titel 7. als geltendes Recht darstellt.

Danach ist der Gutsherr nicht nur als Polizei- und Gerichts-Obrigkeit der Regel nach befugt, Schulzen und Schöppen zur Verwaltung der Gemeinde-Angelegenheiten seiner Gutsunterthanen zu ernennen und solchen in Polizei-Angelegenheiten Anweisungen zu geben, sondern es sind die Unterthanen auch verpflichtet, dem Gutsherrn als Obrigkeit eidlich Gehorsam zu geloben; die Unterthänigkeit wird als gesetzliche Regel vermuthet; der unterthänige Bauer darf ohne Consens des Gutsherrn seinen Hof nicht verkaufen oder verpfänden, er darf auch nicht in Dienst treten oder eine Profession übernehmen oder sich verheirathen ohne Consens des Gutsherrn.

Die Kinder eines unterthänigen Bauern dürfen sich gleichfalls ohne Consens des Gutsherrn weder verheirathen noch vermiethen, und müssen, wenn sie nicht den elterlichen Hof übernehmen, dem Gutsherrn auf dessen Verlangen gegen landüblichen Lohn dienen. Die gutsherrlichen Dienste und Abgaben dürfen vom Gutsherrn nicht willkührlich erhöht werden.

Wesentlich zum Schutze der Gutsunterthanen gereichte hauptsächlich die Bestimmung, daß der Heiraths-Consens der Gutsunterthanen nicht willkührlich versagt werden durfte und daß keine bäuerlichen Stellen eingezogen werden durften. Interessant für die Auffassung der gutsherrlich bäuerlichen Verhältnisse ist eine Vorstellung der Stände von Pommern an Friedrich II. vom 29. Juli 1763. Der König hatte verordnet, es solle „absolut und ohne das geringste Raisonniren alle Leibeigenschaft von Stund an gänzlich abgeschafft werden." Die Stände, deren Eingabe Theil III. S. 99 der Geschichte Friedrich's II. von Preuß abgedruckt ist, stellten nun vor, es bestehe in Pommern keine Leibeigenschaft sondern Gutspflichtigkeit; wenn diese aufgehoben und Freizügigkeit eingeführt werde, so würden sowohl das junge unverständige Volk als die auf Höfen wohnenden Bauern außer Landes oder in die Städte gehn; nur in Folge der Gutspflichtigkeit sei es bisher möglich gewesen, austretende Bauern, auch solche, die sich aus Furcht vor dem Soldaten-Stande geflüchtet hätten, zu reclamiren und ihre Auslieferung von auswärtigen Behörden zu verlangen.

Auf Grund dieser Vorstellung gab Friedrich II. jede durchgreifende Aenderung der Gutsunterthänigkeit in Pommern auf.

Wenn somit auch noch in der Gutsunterthänigkeit des Land-Rechtes bedeutende Reste der Leibeigenschaft erhalten sind, so war doch die Lage der Gutsunterthanen schon in der zweiten Hälfte des 18. Jahrhunderts eine wesentlich andere und bessere, als solche gegen Ende des 17. Jahrhunderts gewesen war. Der beste Beweis dafür ist der, daß in der zweiten Hälfte des 18. Jahrhunderts nicht mehr über das Entlaufen der Unterthanen geklagt wird, während derartige Klagen im 17. Jahrhundert vielfach vorkommen, so z. B.

in der Pommerschen Gesinde-, Bauer- und Schäfer-Ordnung vom 18. December 1670, in der es wörtlich heißt: „die Namen der Entlaufenen sollen von dem Henker an drei und mehr Orten ausgerufen und an den Galgen, Pranger oder Kaak geschlagen werden, weil er als Dieb seiner Obrigkeit die Leibeigenschaft gestohlen hat.“

§. 25.

Wesentliche Aenderungen im Gebiete des eigentlichen Civil-Rechts erfolgten bis zur Abfassung des allgemeinen Landrechts im Preußischen Staate nur wenige, indem die zahlreichen landesherrlichen Verordnungen, welche z. B. in Bezug auf Vormundschaft, Ordnung, Wechselrecht u. s. w. ergingen, meistens nur das bestehende Recht zusammenstellten.

Erwähnungswerth sind hauptsächlich die Verordnung Friedrich Wilhelm's I. vom 5. Januar 1717, durch welche die Lehngüter, soweit der Landesherr Lehnsherr war, mit einer an Stelle der Lehndienste tretenden Abgabe belastet, im Uebrigen aber, jedoch unbeschadet der Rechte der Agnaten und Mitbelehnten, für freies Eigenthum der Vasallen erklärt wurden. Viel wichtiger sind die materiellen Aenderungen, welche durch Einführung des Pfandbriefs-Instituts in der letzten Hälfte der Regierung Friedrich's II. herbeigeführt wurden.

Die Entstehung dieses Instituts ist bekannt. Durch den siebenjährigen Krieg waren namentlich in Schlesien die Gutsbesitzer in große Schulden gestürzt, die allgemeine Creditlosigkeit, welche durch ein den Gutsbesitzern bewilligtes Moratorium noch vermehrt wurde, erschwerte ihnen, die Geldmittel zur Wiederherstellung ihrer Güter geliehn zu erhalten. Angeregt durch die Vorschläge eines Kaufmanns Büring veranlaßte nun der damals noch in Schlesien fungirende Minister von Carmer die Rittergutsbesitzer dieser Provinz durch gemeinschaftliche Verbürgung ihren Credit zu heben. Dies war der Ursprung des Pfandbriefs-Instituts in Schlesien, welches im Jahre 1770 von Friedrich II. bestätigt und noch im 18. Jahrhundert in der Mark, Pommern, Ost- und West-Preußen nachgeahmt wurde.

Die Grundzüge dieses Instituts sind bekannt. Sie beruhn darauf, daß jedem zum Pfandbrief-Verbande gehörigen Gutsbesitzer bis auf einen bestimmten Theil des Taxwerths seines Gutes das Recht zur Aufnahme von Dahrlehn auf Pfandbriefe gegeben ward. Diese Pfandbriefe sind lettres au porteur, welche Seitens der Gläubiger nicht kündbar sind und deren Verzinsung von sämmtlichen Gutsbesitzern des Pfandbrief-Verbandes garantirt ist.

Dieses Institut hat wesentlich dazu beigetragen, den Rittergutsbesitzern auf leichte und billige Weise Credit zu verschaffen und hat dahersf ehr viel zur Hebung der Landes-Cultur, aber auch zu größerer Verschuldung der Rittergüter mitgewirkt. Wichtig ist es aber auch um deßwillen, weil es den größten Einfluß auf Ausbildung des Preußischen Hypothekenrechts gehabt hat. Bei den Pfandbriefen kam nämlich zuerst das Princip zur Anwendung, welches die Haupt-Grundlage des Preußischen Hypothekenrechts bildet, daß nämlich die in das Hypothekenbuch eingetragene Forderung, beim Pfandbriefs-Institut, also die Pfandbriefs-Schuld, allen anderen Forderungen namentlich auch den gesetzlichen Pfand-Rechten vorgeht.

§. 26.

Von Wichtigkeit für das noch jetzt geltende Privatrecht sind geworden die Verordnungen von Friedrich II. über die Nothwendigkeit der Schriftlichkeit der Verträge.

Schon in dem Stempel-Edict am 13. Mai 1766 war lediglich im Stempel-Interesse vorgeschrieben, daß Kauf-, Mieths- und Pacht-Contracte über Immobilien bei Vermeidung der Nullität schriftlich sein sollten. Diese Vorschrift ward nun durch Gesetz vom 8. Februar 1770 auf alle Verträge ohne Unterschied, deren Object über 50 Thlr. betrug, mit Ausschluß allein des depositum miserabile, der Verträge der Kaufleute und einiger ähnlicher Fälle ausgedehnt. Man ging soweit, daß z. B. wer ohne schriftlichen Schuldschein ein Darlehn von mehr als 50 Thlr. gegeben hatte, dasselbe nicht zurückfordern konnte. Die offenbare Ungerechtigkeit, welche hierin lag, veranlaßte, daß nach vielfachen Beschwerden der Unterthanen und Gerichte durch Verordnung vom 10. März 1781 die Folgen der nicht erfolgten Anwendung der Schriftform gemildert wurden, so daß dieselbe blos die Unklagbarkeit, nicht aber die absolute Nullität des Geschäftes zur Folge hatte. In dieser Art ist die Vorschrift der Schriftform der Verträge in das Allgemeine Land-Recht aufgenommen und daher noch gegenwärtig geltendes Recht.

Leider giebt diese Vorschrift noch heutzutage fast täglich Anlaß zu den offenbarsten Verletzungen von Treu und Glauben durch Nichtachtung der blos mündlich geschlossenen Verträge. Nicht leicht wird jetzt noch jemand diese Bestimmung durch den Grund rechtfertigen wollen, welcher bei Erlaß des Stempel-Edicts vom 1766 maßgebend war, weil sie nämlich allerdings geeignet ist, den Abschluß schriftlicher Verträge zu befördern und somit die Einnahme der Stempelsteuer zu vermehren. Was man für jene Vorschrift jetzt noch anführt, ist hauptsächlich, daß durch die Nothwendigkeit des schriftlichen Abschlusses der Verträge die Bestimmtheit des Ausdrucks der Absicht der Parteien herbeigeführt und somit den Streitigkeiten vorgebeugt werde, welche aus der oft zweifelhaften Auslegung mündlicher Verträge entstehen können.

Man darf aber nicht übersehen, wie oft schriftliche Verträge so undeutlich abgefaßt sind, daß sich aus ihnen die wahre Willensmeinung der Parteien durchaus nicht entnehmen läßt, ja daß oft die Worte der schriftlichen Verträge mit der wahren Willensmeinung der Parteien in offenbarem Widerspruche stehen. Erwägt man nun ferner, daß der Mangel der Schriftform täglich Anlaß zur offenbarsten Verletzung von Treu und Glauben giebt, so wird man gewiß den bewährtesten Autoritäten des Preußischen Rechtes, einem Koch und Bornemann beitreten müssen, welche beide, und zwar Bornemann in seinen neuesten Schriften, abweichend von seinen früheren Ansichten, die Nothwendigkeit der Schriftform bei allen Verträgen für eine höchst unglückliche Bestimmung des Preußischen Rechts halten.

§. 27.

Das Princip der möglichsten Bevormundung der Unterthanen durch den Staat spricht sich noch in andern Gesetzen Friedrich's II. aus. So z. B. ward bald nach dem siebenjährigen Kriege der Holz-handel, soweit er sich auf Versorgung der größeren Städte mit Holz bezog, unter Controlle des Staats gestellt und monopolisirt. Ebenso wurden durch die Forstgesetze die Privatforsten so sehr der Controlle der Forstbehörden unterworfen, daß jede freie Verfügung der Gutsbesitzer über ihre Forsten aufhörte. Diese Beschränkungen der Freiheit des Eigenthums sind jedoch durch das Landes-Cultur-Edict vom 9. October 1807 hinweggefallen.

Noch müssen wir aber eines Gesetzes von Friedrich II. erwähnen, welches wesentlichen Einfluß auf unser heutiges Recht gehabt hat. Es ist dies das General-Land-Schul-Reglement vom 12. August 1763, entworfen vom Ober-Consistorial-Rath Hecker, vom Könige selbst durchgesehen und verbessert (Rabe, Bd. I. Abth. II. S. 557). Durch dies Gesetz ward der unbedingte Schulzwang eingeführt, indem verordnet wurde, daß alle Kinder ohne Unterschied, soweit sie nicht Privat-Unterricht genössen, vom vollendeten 5. Lebensjahre ab und zwar der Regel nach bis zum vollendeten 13. oder 14. Lebensjahre die Schule besuchen sollten, und daß die Befolgung dieser Verordnung nöthigenfalls durch Strafen der Eltern oder Vormünder der Kinder erzwungen werden sollte.

Dieser Schulzwang ist aus dem Gesetze vom 12. August 1763 in das Allgemeine Landrecht und demnächst auch in die Cabinets-Ordre vom 14. Mai übergegangen. Er bildet noch jetzt die Grundlage unseres Schulwesens. Vielfach hat man denselben als eine despotische Beschränkung der öffentlichen Freiheit angegriffen, indessen wird man doch wohl anerkennen müssen, daß nur durch ihn es möglich geworden ist, die Schulbildung so allgemein, wie jetzt der Fall ist, auch unter den ärmsten Classen der Nation zu verbreiten.

§. 28.

Von der größten Wichtigkeit für unsern Rechts-Zustand war die Abfassung des Allgemeinen Landrechts.

Es war dies im neuern Europa das erste, alle Zweige des Rechts umfassende, vollständige Gesetzbuch. Das Oestreichische Gesetzbuch, sowie der code Napoléon sind bekanntlich spätern Ursprungs. Die Geschichte der Abfassung des Allgemeinen Landrechts ist bekannt.

Die specielle Ausarbeitung desselben erfolgte unter Leitung des Großkanzlers von Carmer hauptsächlich durch den unermüdlich thätigen Suarez. Der erste Entwurf des Gesetzbuchs wurde in den Jahren 1784 bis 1788 gedruckt, weil der Großkanzler es für zweckmäßig hielt, vor definitiver Einführung des Gesetzbuchs dem Publikum Gelegenheit zu geben, sich darüber zu äußern. In Gemäßheit einer Cabinets-Ordre Friedrich Wilhelm's II. vom 27. August 1786 wurden auch die Stände sämmtlicher Provinzen mit ihrem Gutachten über den Entwurf des Gesetzbuchs gehört und nachdem dasselbe unter Berücksichtigung sämmtlicher eingegangenen Monita überarbeitet war, ward es durch Publications-Patent vom 20. März 1791 unter dem Titel „Allgemeines Gesetzbuch für die Preußischen Staaten“ publicirt, so daß es vom 1. Juni 1792 ab Gesetzeskraft erhalten sollte.

Vor Eintritt dieses Zeitpunktes ward es jedoch durch Cabinets-Ordre vom 18. April 1792 suspendirt, auf Befehl des Königs abermals überarbeitet, und erlangte dann auf Grund des Publications-Patents vom 7. Februar 1794 für die Zeit vom 1. Juni 1794 ab unter dem Namen des Allgemeinen Landrechts Gesetzeskraft.

§. 29.

Es umfaßt sowohl öffentliches als Privat-Recht, einschließlich des Criminal-Rechts. Die materiellen Bestimmungen desselben enthalten im Ganzen nur wenig Neues. Der König ist als unumschränkter Souverän aufgefaßt, dem das Gesetzgebungs- und Besteuerungs-Recht, sowie das Recht, Krieg zu erklären und Frieden zu schließen, allein zusteht.

Von einer Beschränkung des Königs durch Rechte der Stände ist eben so wenig die Rede, als von den Verpflichtungen des Staats gegenüber dem Deutschen Reiche.

Letztere hatten in der That seit dem Beginn der Regierung Friedrich's II. nur noch der Form nach bestanden; das Kirchengebet für den Römischen Kaiser, welches von Alters her in ganz Deutschland hergebracht war, war auf Befehl Friedrich's II. bereits im Jahre 1750 in allen Landestheilen abgeschafft worden, so daß auch dieses Zeichen der alten Oberherrlichkeit des Kaisers lange vor Abfassung des Allgemeinen Landrechts beseitigt war.

Die Machtvollkommenheit des Königs ist aber im Allgemeinen Landrecht als eine durch Gesetze geregelte aufgefaßt und daher jeder Machtspruch, d. h. jedes willkührliche Eingreifen des Königs in Privatrechte für unzulässig erklärt, eine Bestimmung, die, wie wir gesehen haben, durchaus dem seit den ältesten Zeiten in der Mark geltenden Rechte entspricht und auch schon in den im Jahre 1748 erschienenen Codex Fridericianus aufgenommen war.

Vom Adel heißt es im Thl. II. Tit. 9. des Landrechts, daß er zur Bekleidung von Aemtern vorzüglich geeignet sei.

Auch diese Bestimmung entsprach dem zu jener Zeit geltenden Rechte, denn seit Anfang des 18. Jahrhunderts wurden Officier-Stellen, außer bei der Artillerie, in der Regel nur an Edelleute gegeben. Ebenso waren sämmtliche Minister und die ersten Präsidenten der Provinzial-Collegien immer Edelleute. Die Bevorzugung des Adels bei Besetzung der höhern Beamten-Stellen hatte sich erst seit der Aufhebung der landständischen Rechte ausgebildet; so lange diese Rechte noch in Kraft bestanden, hatten die Landesherren vielfach die höchsten Beamten-Stellen mit Bürgerlichen besetzt, vielleicht gerade um ein Gegengewicht gegen die Macht des in den Ständen vorwiegenden Adels zu haben. Gerade mit dem Aufhören der Macht der Stände aber hatte der Adel sich vorzugsweise der Beamten-Carriere gewidmet und allmälig durch Gewohnheit gewissermaßen ein ausschließliches Recht auf die höchsten Beamten-Posten erworben. Unter den neun Mitgliedern des Staatsraths z. B., welche diese Behörde bei deren Stiftung im Jahre 1604 bildeten, waren vier Bürgerliche, während unter Friedrich Wilhelm I. und Friedrich II. nicht ein einziger Bürgerlicher sich im Staatsrath befand.

Die Ehe zwischen Mannspersonen von Adel und Frauenspersonen vom Bauern- und niedern Bürgerstande ist im Landrecht für absolut nichtig erklärt, was eine wesentliche Abweichung vom frühern Rechte enthält, welches, wie wir gesehen haben, als Folge der Eingehung einer derartigen Ehe blos den Verlust des Adels des heirathenden Edelmanns eintreten ließ.

Es bedarf wohl nicht des Nachweises, daß diese zum Glück für das praktische Leben ziemlich einflußlose Neuerung des Landrechts auf einem tiefen Verkennen der religiösen und sittlichen Bedeutung der Ehe beruht; gewiß mit Recht hatte die christliche Kirche von Anfang an selbst eine Ehe zwischen Freien und Sclaven als gültig angesehen, — allerdings im Widerspruch mit den aus der Zeit des Heidenthums stammenden Satzungen des Römischen Rechts, — unmöglich kann man nach den Grundsätzen der christlichen Kirche eine Ehe wegen eines bloßen Standes-Unterschieds als nichtig ansehen; dies ist nur möglich, wenn man in der Ehe Nichts sieht, als ein bloßes Staats-Institut, wenn man ihr gar keine sittliche oder religiöse Bedeutung beilegt. Es wird ferner im Landrecht das bestehende Verbot des Besitzes und Erwerbes von Rittergütern durch Bürgerliche erwähnt; der Rittergutsbesitzer wird als Inhaber der Patrimonial-Gerichtsbarkeit und als Orts-Obrigkeit in Bezug auf die ländlichen Gemeinden bezeichnet.

Die Gutsunterthänigkeit wird durchaus dem bestehenden Rechte gemäß dargestellt, ebenso die Gewerbs- und Zunft-Privilegien des Bürgerstandes; auf die bestehende Militair-Verfassung mit ihren harten Strafen für unbefugte Auswanderung und noch mehr für Desertion wird wiederholt hingedeutet.

Was das Kirchenrecht betrifft, so spricht das Allgemeine Landrecht im 11. Titel des 2. Theils das Princip der unbedingten Gewissens- und Religions-Freiheit aus, unterscheidet jedoch zwischen anerkannten und blos geduldeten Religions-Gesellschaften, macht die Stiftung einer neuen Religions-Gesellschaft von der Genehmigung des Staats abhängig und hält allen Kirchen gegenüber das Oberaufsichts-Recht des Staats in ziemlich weiter Ausdehnung aufrecht.

Auch im Gebiete des eigentlichen Civilrechts, namentlich also des Personen- und Familien-Rechts, der Lehre vom Besitz und Eigenthum, in dem Obligationen- und Erbrecht, sowie dem See-, Handels- und Wechselrecht haben die Verfasser des Landrechts im

Wesentlichen nur die Bestimmungen des bereits geltenden Rechts codificirt und nur wenige absichtliche Aenderungen vorgenommen.

§. 30.

Die wesentlichste unter diesen Aenderungen ist die auf das Hypothekar-Recht bezügliche. Sie besteht bekanntlich darin, daß nach Preußischem Recht Hypotheken nur durch Eintragung in Hypothekenbücher, deren formelle Einrichtung bereits durch die Hypotheken-Ordnung von 1783 geordnet war, rechtsgültig bestellt werden können. Die großen Vorzüge, welche dieses Preußische Hypothekenrecht vor den gemeinrechtlichen Bestimmungen hat, sind anerkannt. Freilich läßt sich nicht leugnen, daß dasselbe den Gerichten eine außerordentliche Arbeitslast aufbürdet und dem Publikum große Kosten und Weitläufigkeiten verursacht, aber dieser Nachtheil wird mehr als aufgewogen dadurch, daß Nichts so sehr geeignet ist, den Real-Credit der Grundbesitzer zu begründen, als gerade die Preußische Hypotheken-Gesetzgebung. Unstreitig hat letztere daher wesentlich zur Hebung der Landes-Cultur unseres Vaterlandes beigetragen.

Das Erforderniß der Schriftlichkeit der Verträge ist, wie bereits erwähnt, hauptsächlich aus der Verordnung von 1770 in das Landrecht übergegangen.

Auch im Gebiete des Criminal-Rechts giebt das Allgemeine Landrecht im Wesentlichen nur die Bestimmungen, welche zur Zeit seiner Abfassung bereits in der Praxis der Preußischen Gerichte Geltung erworben hatten.

Die sogenannten qualificirten Todesarten, z. B. das Rädern für Raubmörder, das lebendig Verbrennen für Mordbrenner, sind im Landrecht noch beibehalten. Letztere Strafe ist zuletzt an zwei Brandstiftern, welche in Teltow wiederholt Feuer angelegt hatten, im Jahre 1813 dicht bei Berlin vollstreckt, die Strafe des Räderns ist bekanntlich noch weit länger in Gebrauch geblieben, und haben wir den gänzlichen Wegfall dieser qualificirten Todesarten erst dem Strafgesetzbuch vom 14. April 1851 zu verdanken.

Die verstümmelnden Strafen kennt jedoch bereits das Allgemeine Landrecht nicht mehr. Die Todesstrafe für den Diebstahl, welche bekanntlich in dem hochgebildeten England noch in unserm Jahrhundert häufig vollstreckt wurde, ist im Landrecht gänzlich abgeschafft; überhaupt ist die Strafe des Diebstahls und Betrugs, der beiden am meisten vorkommenden Verbrechen, wenn man von der allerdings harten Strafe des vierten Diebstahls absieht, im Landrecht bedeutend milder als in dem Französischen code pénal und sogar milder als in dem jetzt geltenden Strafgesetzbuch vom 14. April 1851. Die Prügelstrafe ist nur für wenige Fälle beibehalten, erst durch die nach Erlaß des Landrechts gegebene Circular=Verordnung vom 26. Februar 1799 ward sie für eine Reihe Verbrechen, namentlich Diebstahl und Raub, unter Aufhebung der Bestimmungen des Allgemeinen Landrechts wieder eingeführt.

Fassen wir den materiellen Inhalt des Allgemeinen Landrechts zusammen, so ist dasselbe im Wesentlichen nur eine Codification des zur Zeit seiner Abfassung geltenden materiellen Rechts. Wenn dies in manchen Punkten, z. B. hinsichtlich der Vorschriften über das Verhältniß der Guts=Unterthänigkeit, der Stände=Unterschiede u. s. w. uns durchaus mißfällt, so dürfen wir doch keineswegs die Fehler des materiellen Rechts den Verfassern des Landrechts zur Last legen, denn diese waren nicht Gesetzgeber in dem Sinne, daß es in ihrer Macht gestanden hätte, irgend etwas Wesentliches am bestehenden Rechte zu ändern. Was z. B. die Bestimmungen über die gutsherrlich=bäuerlichen Verhältnisse und namentlich das Verhältniß der Unterthänigkeit betrifft, so ist erwiesen, daß Suarez die Bestimmungen des Landrechtsn icht billigte, sondern einem der Monenten beistimmte, welcher die Aufhebung der Unterthänigkeit fast ganz in der Art, wie solche nachher durch das Edict vom 9. October 1807 erfolgt ist, vorschlug. Aber Suarez mußte das Landrecht dem bestehenden Recht und nicht seiner eigenen Ueberzeugung gemäß redigiren.

Durch den Charakter der Zeit, in welcher das Landrecht entstanden ist, ist es ferner zu erklären, daß dasselbe den Wirkungskreis der Staatsbehörden zum Nachtheile der freien Selbstbestimmung der Einzelnen auf's Aeußerste ausdehnt. Dies zeigt sich namentlich im Vormundschafts-Recht, in welchem die Thätigkeit der Vormünder fast ganz von den Anweisungen des Vormundschafts-Gerichts abhängig gemacht ist.

Was die Form des Landrechts betrifft, so ist man gegenwärtig wohl darüber einig, daß dasselbe in Folge eines mißlungenen Strebens nach allgemeiner Verständlichkeit im Allgemeinen breit, weitschweifig und häufig eben wegen zu großer Breite unklar und unbestimmt ist.

§. 31.

Ehe wir noch auf die gänzliche Umwandlung unserer Gesetzgebung und Verwaltung in den Jahren 1806—1813 kommen, müssen wir einen Blick auf das Militair- und Abgaben-Wesen werfen, wie solches sich während des 18. Jahrhunderts ausgebildet hatte.

Die Armee hatte seit ihrer Bildung durch den großen Kurfürsten bis zum Jahre 1733 aus geworbenen Truppen bestanden. Eine eigentliche Aushebung hatte bis zu jenem Jahre nur für die Miliz bestanden, welche nur zur Bewachung der Gränze und der Festungen bestimmt, außer Landes nicht zu dienen brauchte und auch nur 5000 Mann stark war.

Bei der großen Vermehrung der Armee unter Friedrich Wilhelm I. reichte jedoch die freiwillige Werbung nicht mehr aus, um die Armee vollzählig zu erhalten. Es ward daher durch Cabinets-Ordre vom 1. und 18. Mai 1733 eine allgemeine Aushebung für das stehende Heer unter Anweisung eines bestimmten Cantons für jeden Truppentheil vorgeschrieben. Nach dem ursprünglichen Canton-Reglement vom 15. September 1733 waren nur der Adel und diejenigen Söhne bürgerlichen Standes, welche ein sicheres Vermögen von 10,000 Thlr. hatten, kantonfrei. Es wurden jedoch mehr und mehr Ausnahmen von dieser fast allgemeinen Militairpflichtigkeit gemacht. Nicht nur die Bewohner der meisten größeren Städte, z. B. Berlin, Potsdam, Magdeburg, Breslau, wurden militairfrei, sondern auch die Söhne aller Beamten, mit Ausnahme der niedern Subaltern-Beamten, ferner die älteren Söhne ansäßiger Bauern, Kossäthen u. s. w., so daß nur der ärmste und ungebildetste Theil der Nation militairpflichtig blieb. Neben der Aushebung im Inlande blieb noch die Werbung im Ausland bestehen, welche der Armee die schlechtesten Elemente zuführte. Man scheute sich auch nicht, aus den Gefängnissen verurtheilte Diebe und Betrüger zu nehmen und in die Armee zu reihen.

Die Dienstzeit betrug 20 Jahre, indessen war der Soldat, wenigstens der Inländer, bei welchem man Desertion nicht zu befürchten brauchte, während des größern Theils dieser Dienstzeit beurlaubt. Der Kriegsminister von Boyen berechnet in seiner „Darstellung der Grundsätze der alten und gegenwärtigen Preußischen Kriegs-Verfassung, Berlin 1817“ die Zeit, während deren in der Regel ein Soldat während seiner 20jährigen Dienstzeit wirklich bei den Fahnen stand, für den Cavalleristen auf 2 Jahre 7 Monat, für den Infanteristen auf 21½ Monat.

Was die Stellung der Soldaten betrifft, so war diese in pecuniärer Beziehung weit besser, als sie jetzt ist, denn der Sold des gemeinen Soldaten war mit Rücksicht auf den jetzt so sehr gefallenen Geldwerth unter Friedrich Wilhelm I. und Friedrich II. weit höher als solcher jetzt ist, außerdem aber hatte der Soldat durch die häufige Beurlaubung weit mehr Gelegenheit, sich selbst etwas zu erwerben, als gegenwärtig. Hierdurch erklärt es sich, daß ein großer Theil, vielleicht die Hälfte der Soldaten zu Friedrich's II. Zeit verheirathet war, während es jetzt keinem Soldaten möglich sein würde, von seinem Solde und etwanigen Neben-Verdienste mit Frau und Kind zu leben.

Aber in jeder andern Beziehung war die Lage des gemeinen Soldaten desto schlimmer. Man hat diese Lage wohl nicht mit Unrecht als eine Knechtschaft der schlimmsten Art bezeichnet. An ein Avancement des gemeinen Soldaten zu einem Offizier war nicht zu denken, da der Adel das ausschließliche Recht zur Besetzung der Offizier-Stellen hatte. Die barbarische Strenge der Disciplin namentlich das häufige Spießruthenlaufen sind allgemein bekannt; um diese Härte der Disciplin erklärlich zu finden, muß man berücksichtigen, daß die Werbung im Auslande die rohesten Subjecte unserer

Armee zuführte, und daß überhaupt in jener Zeit, in welcher, wie uns das bekannte Prügel-Mandat lehrt, das Prügeln der Bauern und Knechte an der Tagesordnung war und die Leibeigenschaft sich kaum noch in die Gutsunterthänigkeit umgewandelt hatte, eine nach unseren Begriffen äußerst harte Behandlung des aus den niedrigsten Ständen zusammengesetzten Heeres sehr natürlich war. Wie sehr schon im 18. Jahrhundert ein großer Theil der Soldaten die Härte ihres Looses fühlten, das zeigen nicht nur die häufigen Desertionen und die vielfachen Entweichungen cantonpflichtiger Personen aus dem Lande aus Furcht vor der Aushebung zum Militair, sondern auch z. B. das Edict vom 4. December 1764 (Mylius N. C. C. M. B. 3. S. 527), durch welches man für nöthig gehalten hatte, bei der härtesten Strafe den Militairpflichtigen zu verbieten, sich durch Verstümmlung des Daumens zum Kriegsdienst untüchtig zu machen. Die Zahl der Armee war wenigstens unter Friedrich II. im Verhältniß zur Bevölkerung des Staats weit größer als jetzt. Sie betrug gegen Ende dieser Regierung bei einer Bevölkerung von 5,200,000 Seelen etwa 190,000 Mann. Nach diesem Verhältnisse müßte unsere Armee jetzt bei einer Bevölkerung von 17,400,000 Menschen 550—600,000 Mann betragen, während das stehende Heer mit Reserve und erstem Aufgebot der Landwehr doch nur 350,000 Mann stark ist.

§. 32.

Von den Steuern war die bedeutendste die Grundsteuer, welche Contribution, auch General-Hufenschloß, Landsteuer, Hufensteuer genannt wurde. Sie war in den ältern Provinzen, wie wir gesehn haben, durch den großen Kurfürsten als dauernde Abgabe eingeführt, ward in diesen Provinzen wiederholt, namentlich in den Jahren 1717, 1730 u. 1733 revidirt, und von Friedrich II. auch in Schlesien und Westpreußen eingeführt. In einigen Provinzen, namentlich Brandenburg und Pommern, waren die Rittergüter bis auf die sogenannten Lehnpferdegelder steuerfrei, in anderen namentlich Schlesien und Preußen waren sie besteuert. In Schlesien z. B. hatte Friedrich II. im Jahre 1744 die Steuer in der Art eingeführt, daß von den Bauerngütern 34 Procent, von den Rittergütern 28⅓ Procent, von geistlichen und Stiftsgütern 50 Procent des Rein-Ertrages als Steuer gezahlt werden sollten.

Seit Anfang der Regierung Friedrich's II. bis zum jetzigen Augenblick ist die Grundsteuer in Pommern, Brandenburg, Schlesien und Ostpreußen nicht erhöhet worden.

Von den indirecten Steuern war die erheblichüe die Accise, gleichfalls schon vom großen Kurfürsten dauernd eingeführt. Sie ward unter den spätern Regierungen wiederholt in einzelnen Bestimmungen modificirt, und in den neu erworbenen Provinzen eingeführt. Durchgreifend war die Aenderung, welche Friedrich II. in Accise- und Zoll-Sachen im Jahre 1766 durch Einführung der sogenannten Regie vornahm, indem er namentlich den Handel mit Tabak und Kaffee monopolisirte, doch wurden das Tabaks- und Kaffee-Monopol, welche die größte Unzufriedenheit hervorgerufen hatten, bereits im Jahre 1787 von Friedrich Wilhelm II. wieder aufgehoben.

Die Stempel-Steuer bestand gleichfalls seit der Regierung des großen Kurfürsten, welcher sie im Jahre 1682 eingeführt hatte; das Salzmonopol bestand seit dem Jahre 1725. — Interessant ist die Frage: ob die Steuerlast in unserm Vaterlande gegenwärtig höher oder geringer ist als sie während des 18. Jahrhunderts war.

Der Gesammtbetrag der Staats-Einnahmen betrug gegen Ende der Regierung Friedrich Wilhelm's I. bei 2,300,000 Einwohnern 7,400,000 Thaler, gegen Ende der Regierung Friedrich's II. bei 5,900,000 Einwohnern etwa 20 Millionen Thaler (Preuß Geschichte Friedrich's II. Band 4. S. 292 ff.), so daß also auf den Kopf der Bevölkerung jährlich unter Friedrich Wilhelm I. etwa 3 Thaler, unter Friedrich II. etwa 4 Thaler Staats-Einnahme kamen. Gegenwärtig (1860) rechnet man auf den Kopf der Bevölkerung bei einer Einwohnerzahl von 17,400,000 Seelen und einem jährlichen Budget von 110 Millionen Thaler 7 bis 8 Thaler jährliche Staats-Einnahme. Man darf jedoch nicht außer Acht lassen, daß bis 1806 sehr viele Ausgaben von den Gemeinden und Kreisen oder Einzelnen bestritten wurden, welche jetzt dem Staate obliegen und das Staats-Budget vermehren. Dies ist z. B. mit fast sämmtlichen Ausgaben für die Justiz der Fall, denn diese Ausgaben wurden bis zu jener Zeit in Bezug auf sämmtliche städtische und Patrimonial-Gerichte lediglich von den Städten oder Patrimonial-Gerichts-Herrn und auch bei den Königlichen Gerichten zum größten Theil aus der den Richtern als Theil der Besoldung dienenden Sportel-Einnahme bestritten, während sie jetzt vom Staate getragen werden und im jetzigen Budget das Justiz-Ministerium mit einer Einnahme und Ausgabe von circa 10 Millionen Thalern aufgeführt ist.

Ferner muß man berücksichtigen, daß bis 1806 noch neben den eigentlichen Steuern eine Menge Leistungen für den Staat, z. B. der Vorspann, der Unterhalt der Land- und Heer-Straßen von den Unterthanen unentgeltlich verrichtet wurden und, was wohl die Hauptsache ist, daß sich der National-Wohlstand seit dem 18. Jahrhundert außerordentlich vermehrt hat, der Geldwerth aber gesunken ist.

Seit 1740 hat sich der Geldwerth der Grundstücke im Preußischen Staate mindestens verfünffacht; hat er sich ja doch von 1815 bis jetzt mehr als verdreifacht. Da nun die Grundsteuer in Brandenburg, Pommern und Ostpreußen seit der Regierung Friedrich Wilhelm's I. in Schlesien seit 1744 nicht erhöhet ist, so kommt man zu dem Resultate, daß dieselbe um 1750 in den erwähnten Provinzen im Verhältniß zur damaligen Rein-Einnahme der Grundbesitzer mindestens viermal so hoch war, wie sie jetzt ist. Sieht man aber von dieser einzelnen Steuer ab und faßt das gesammte Abgaben-Wesen ins Auge, so wird man nicht zweifeln können, daß die Abgaben in dem Zeitraume von der zweiten Hälfte des 17. Jahrhunderts bis 1806 in unserm Vaterlande weit höher und für die Nation drückender waren, als sie jetzt sind, schon um deßwillen, weil 3 Thaler Steuern auf den Kopf unter Friedrich Wilhelm I. und 4 Thaler unter Friedrich II. im Verhältnisse zu dem damaligen Geldwerth und Nationalwohlstand ein höherer Betrag waren, als jetzt 7—8 Thaler auf den Kopf sind.

§. 33.

Bei den indirecten Abgaben herrschte im vorigen Jahrhundert in unserm Vaterlande wie fast in ganz Europa das Mercantil-System. Man suchte auf alle Weise die Ausfuhr von rohen Producten und die Einfuhr von Manufactur-Waaren zu beschränken, um die inländischen Fabriken zu begünstigen und das Geld im Lande zu behalten.

Schon der große Kurfürst hatte im Jahre 1644 die Ausfuhr von Wolle verboten; er verbot 1650 auch die Ausfuhr von Flachs und Hanf; diese Verbote wurden im 18. Jahrhundert wiederholt erneuert, namentlich in den Jahren 1719, 1766 und 1774 das Verbot der Wollenausfuhr, auf welche durch die letztgedachte Verordnung vom 3. April 1774 von Friedrich II. sogar Todesstrafe gesetzt wurde.

Auch die Getreide-Ausfuhr war zum großen Schaden der Landwirthschaft schon seit der Zeit des großen Kurfürsten vielfach beschränkt und die Einfuhr der meisten ausländischen Manufactur-Waaren schon seit Friedrich Wilhelm's I. Regierung geradezu verboten.

Wenn nach dem heutigen Standpunct der National-Oekonomie derartige Verbote als durchaus nachtheilig erscheinen, so dürfen wir doch nicht vergessen, daß man im vorigen Jahrhundert eben andere Grundsätze der National-Oekonomie hatte, als man jetzt hat; wenn es uns aber mit Recht als eine furchtbare Härte erscheint, daß Friedrich II. auf die Wollausfuhr Todesstrafe setzte, — welche Strafe übrigens gewiß nie in Anwendung gebracht ist, — so mögen wir auch erwägen, daß noch gegenwärtig unsere Zollgesetze wenigstens in einer Beziehung eine schreiende Härte enthalten.

Während es nämlich nach allgemeinen Rechts-Grundsätzen verboten ist, auf einen fliehenden Dieb zu schießen und während namentlich der Forstbeamte nicht befugt ist, auf einen fliehenden Holz- oder Wilddieb zu schießen, ist es doch nach §. 2a. des Gesetzes vom 28. Juni 1834 über den Waffengebrauch der Grenzbeamten den letztern noch jetzt erlaubt, auf fliehende Schmuggler zu schießen, so daß also die Schmuggler in dieser Beziehung schlimmer als die Diebe behandelt werden.

§. 34.

Fassen wir nun den Zustand des Preußischen Staats vom Jahre 1806 zusammen, so finden wir, daß die Macht des Königs eine in Wirklichkeit völlig absolute war, daß jedoch fast alle auf der frühern Ständischen Verfassung beruhenden Rechts-Verhältnisse, namentlich die kastenartige Trennung der Stände, die Vorrechte des Adels in Bezug auf den Besitz von Rittergütern und hinsichtlich der Besetzung von Offizier-Stellen und Aemtern und die Zunft- und Gewerbs-Privilegien des Bürgerstandes seit dem 17. Jahrhundert im Wesentlichen unverändert geblieben waren, daß der Bauernstand sich der Regel nach in einem Zustande der Guts-Unterthänigkeit befand, welcher sich nicht sehr von dem der Leibeigenschaft unterschied, daß die directen Steuern viel höher wie jetzt und auf die einzelnen Stände und Provinzen höchst ungleich vertheilt waren, daß die indirecten Steuern auf dem Principe des alten Mercantil-Systems beruhten und daß endlich die Militair-Pflicht mit entsetzlicher Härte fast blos auf den niedern Ständen lastete.

Fast alle die Mißbräuche, welche in Frankreich im Jahre 1789 zum Ausbruch der Revolution führten, bestanden somit bis 1806 auch in Preußen. Wenn in Frankreich in Folge der hohen Staatsschulden und der Verschwendung des Hofes der Abgabendruck vielleicht größer war, als in Preußen, so war dafür die Militairpflichtigkeit in Preußen entschieden weit drückender als in Frankreich.

Doch in zwei Beziehungen waren in unserm Vaterlande die Zustände besser als in Frankreich, einmal nämlich waren bei uns Hof, Adel, Geistlichkeit und Beamtenstand nicht so demoralisirt und daher auch nicht so verachtet als in Frankreich, und sodann war die geistige und moralische Bildung der Nation in Preußen im Allgemeinen eine höhere als in Frankreich.

In beiden Beziehungen muß man das Hauptverdienst wohl der großen geistigen und sittlichen Bewegung zuschreiben, welche durch die Lutherische Reformation in unserm Vaterlande hervorgerufen war.

§. 35.

Ganz anders freilich als in Deutschland und Frankreich hatten sich die Verhältnisse in England entwickelt. Dort war seit dem Mittelalter die parlamentarische Verfassung geblieben, es hatte daher der Adel, zu welchem man sowohl die im Oberhause vertretene nobility als die im Unterhause vorherrschende gentry rechnen muß, seine verfassungsmäßigen Rechte bewahrt; Freiheit, Bildung und Wohlstand der Nation hatten sich bei dieser Verfassung in einer weit ausgedehnteren Weise als auf dem Festlande Europa's entwickelt. Zu diesem exceptionell glücklichen Zustande Englands hatte wesentlich mitgewirkt, daß das Land in Folge seiner insularen Lage es nicht nöthig hatte, eine so große stehende Armee zu unterhalten, wie die Staaten des Festlandes, daß also der Umstand, welcher auf dem Festlande am meisten zur Begründung des Absolutismus beitrug, nämlich die Existenz großer stehender Heere in England hinwegfiel, außerdem aber muß man bei Vergleichung der Zustände Englands mit denen der übrigen Staaten Europa's berücksichtigen, daß die socialen und Stände-Verhältnisse in England schon im Mittelalter ganz andere geworden waren, als z. B. in unserm Vaterlande.

Die Leibeigenschaft hatte in England hauptsächlich durch den Einfluß der christlichen Kirche schon im 15. Jahrhundert aufgehört, die Ablösung der Natural-Dienste und Frohnden hatte bereits im 16. Jahrhundert stattgefunden, die Gerichtsbarkeit und Polizei-Gewalt war nie in der Ausdehnung wie in Deutschland aus den Händen des Landesherrn in die des Adels und der Städte übergegangen. Der Adel war in England zwar immer ein bevorrechteter Stand geblieben, aber niemals eine abgeschlossene Kaste geworden, wie dies in Deutschland durch die eigenthümliche Ansicht von Mißheirathen der Fall war; von dem Rechte der Nobilitirung, welches in der Mark zuerst der große Kurfürst in sehr beschränkter Weise ausübte, hatten die Englischen Könige immerfort und in größter Ausdehnung Gebrauch gemacht, was gleichfalls viel dazu beigetragen haben mag, daß in England niemals Adel und Bürgerschaft sich so schroff wie in Deutschland geschieden haben.

Alle diese Verhältnisse haben zusammengewirkt, den Uebergang von der feudalen Verfassungs-Form des Mittelalters zur constitutionellen Regierungs-Form der Neuzeit in England mehr als in irgend einem Staate des Festlandes zu erleichtern und zugleich zu bewirken, daß die parlamentarische Verfassung Englands Seitens der dortigen privilegirten Klassen niemals zu einer eigentlichen Bedrückung der Nation gemißbraucht ist.

§. 36.

Wohin dagegen bei den in Deutschland während des Mittelalters entstandenen socialen Verhältnissen das Festhalten an den Verfassungen des 16. Jahrhunderts hätte führen müssen, zeigt uns das Beispiel Mecklenburgs. Dort haben die aus den Rittergutsbesitzern und den Abgeordneten der Städte zusammengesetzten Stände ihre verfassungsmäßigen Rechte seit dem 16. Jahrhundert im Wesentlichen behauptet, der Versuch des Umsturzes der alten Verfassung, den der Großherzog Leopold im 18. Jahrhundert machte, ward durch den Widerstand der Stände nach langen Unruhen, welche zu einer jahrelangen Besetzung des Landes durch Reichstruppen führten, beseitigt, aber leider ist die bestehende Verfassung von den bevorrechteten Ständen in einer kaum glaublichen Weise zur Unterdrückung der Masse des Volks gemißbraucht worden.

Die freien Bauern, deren im 15. und der ersten Hälfte des 16. Jahrhunderts in Mecklenburg wohl nicht weniger als in der Mark gewesen sein mögen, wurden während der zweiten Hälfte des 16. und während des 17. Jahrhunderts fast alle von den Rittergutsbesitzern ausgekauft und ihre Höfe zu den Rittergütern geschlagen. Gegenwärtig zerfällt das Land in das Domanium, d. i. den Domänenbesitz des Landesherrn, die ritterschaftlichen Besitzungen und die Städte mit ihren Kämmerei-Gütern, sowie eine kleine Anzahl Klostergüter. Seit mehr als 50 Jahren sind Bürgerliche zum Besitze von Rittergütern zugelassen. In den Städten aber herrscht noch der schärfste Zunftzwang; die Leibeigenschaft ist zwar nominell im Jahre 1818 aufgehoben, indessen besteht das Unterthänigkeits-Verhältniß der Gutseinsassen in solcher Ausdehnung, daß dasselbe sich wenig von der Leibeigenschaft unterscheidet. So z. B. ist die Eingehung der Ehe des Gutsunterthanen von der Einwilligung des Gutsherrn abhängig und diese Einwilligung kann willkührlich versagt werden und wird sehr häufig versagt. Die Folge davon ist, daß auf den ritterschaftlichen Besitzungen eine Immoralität herrscht, wie sie selbst in heidnischen Ländern glücklicher Weise nur höchst selten vorkommt. In manchen ritterschaftlichen Orten sollen Jahre lang keine andere als uneheliche Kinder geboren sein.

Nach dem officiellen Mecklenburgischen Staats-Kalender für 1860 kam im Jahre 1859 in Mecklenburg-Schwerin ein uneheliches Kind auf noch nicht ganz vier eheliche Kinder, ein Verhältniß, wie es bei der Landbevölkerung wohl nirgends weiter in Europa vorkommen möchte. Dabei ist zu bemerken, daß die Zahl der Einwohner des Domaniums 205,000, die der ritterschaftlichen Besitzungen 136,000 Seelen beträgt; wollte man letztere Besitzungen für sich allein betrachten, so würde man finden, daß die Zahl der unehelichen Geburten bei Weitem die der ehelichen überwiegt. Und doch ist Mecklenburg nur schwach bevölkert, es zählt nur 2220 Einwohner auf die Quadratmeile, es gehört zu den fruchtbarsten Ländern Deutschlands und hat überdies eine äußerst günstige Lage für den Handel, indem es auf der einen Seite an die Ostsee, auf der andern an die Elbe grenzt.

Die Erschwerung der Ehen durch die Gutsherren kann daher gewiß nicht durch die Besorgniß vor Uebervölkerung entschuldigt werden, sie ist auch nicht neuerdings entstanden, sondern noch ein Rest der alten Leibeigenschaft. Im Alterthum hatte man den Sclaven überhaupt für rechtlos und daher zur Eingehung einer Ehe für unfähig erachtet; die Folge, welche dies für die Moralität der Sclaven-Bevölkerung hatte, drückten schon die Römer durch den Spruch aus: „impudicitia in servo necessitas."

Wie im Alterthum die Sclaverei, jedoch in geringerem Grade, hatte im Mittelalter die Leibeigenschaft, welche im Grunde nur eine gemilderte Form der Sclaverei ist, zur Demoralisation einer zahlreichen Classe des Volks beigetragen, und hatten daher schon im

Mittelalter nicht blos die christliche Kirche, sondern auch die gebildetesten Laien z. B. der Verfasser des Sachsenspiegels in Buch III. Artikel 42 anerkannt, daß die Leibeigenschaft ein offenbares Unrecht sei und der Lehre des Christenthums widerstreite. Daß daher noch jetzt in Mecklenburg Zustände, wie so eben erwähnt ist, stattfinden, ist im höchsten Grade zu beklagen im Interesse nicht nur von Mecklenburg, sondern von ganz Deutschland. Die Abhängigkeit der Gutsunterthanen von den Gutsherren ist noch heutzutage in Mecklenburg strenger, als sie in irgend einer Provinz Preußens seit den von uns im §. 24. erwähnten Gesetzen Friedrich's II. gewesen ist. Es sind aber die traurigen Zustände Mecklenburgs vorzugsweise die Folge davon, daß dort sich die alte ständische Verfassung seit dem 16. Jahrhundert behauptet hat. Schätzen wir uns in Preußen daher glücklich, daß die seit der Zeit des großen Kurfürsten bei uns bestehende unumschränkte Gewalt unserer Fürsten das Land nicht nur vor der Unterdrückung durch mächtige Nachbarn, wie sie Polens Schicksal gewesen ist, sondern auch vor solchen innern Zuständen bewahrt hat, wie wir sie noch heutigen Tages in Mecklenburg sehen.

§. 37.

Durch die Katastrophe des Jahres 1806 wurde nun eine totale Umänderung der ganzen socialen Gesetzgebung unseres Staats herbeigeführt, beinahe so groß, als die, welche in Frankreich im Jahre 1789 stattgefunden hatte.

Wir wollen die Hauptbestimmungen der in den Jahren 1806 bis 1813 erschienenen Gesetze kurz zusammenfassen. Nachdem schon während des Krieges noch im Jahre 1806 durch Cabinets-Ordre jedem Soldaten ohne Unterschied des Standes die Aussicht auf Beförderung zum Offizier eröffnet und dadurch das ausschließliche Recht des Adels zu Offizier-Stellen aufgehoben war, erschien bald nach Beendigung des Krieges das Landes-Cultur-Edict vom 9. October 1807. Hervorgegangen aus der Erwägung, daß „die vorhandenen Beschränkungen theils im Besitz und Genuß des Grundeigenthums, theils in den persönlichen Verhältnissen des Landarbeiters der Wiederherstellung der Cultur eine große Kraft entziehen“ erklärte dies

Edict sämmtliche Einwohner des Staats, mit Ausnahme der wenigen Mennoniten, welche durch ihre Religion an der vollen Erfüllung ihrer Bürgerpflichten verhindert seien, für befähigt zum eigenthümlichen und Pfandbesitz jeder Art von unbeweglichen Grundstücken, es erleichterte ferner dem Grundbesitzer jede Art der Disposition über sein Eigenthum und hob die Gutsunterthänigkeit vom Martinitage 1810 ab für ewige Zeiten auf, so daß es von Martini 1810 ab im Preußischen Staate nur noch freie Leute geben sollte. Durch letztere Bestimmung ward die Pflicht des Gutsunterthans, sich vom Gutsherrn den Consens zur Verheirathung oder zum Antritt eines Dienstes, Uebernahme eines Gewerbes rc. zu erbitten, aufgehoben; es fiel somit der letzte Rest der Leibeigenschaft hinweg und ward die persönliche Freiheit aller Staatsbürger in Preußen, hoffentlich für alle Zeiten begründet.

Durch die ersterwähnte Bestimmung war das ausschließliche Recht des Adels zum Besitz von Rittergütern, zugleich aber auch die Verpflichtung der Rittergutsbesitzer zur Wiederbesetzung herrenlos werdender Bauergüter aufgehoben.

Durch das Edict zur Beförderung der Landes-Cultur vom 14. September 1811, sowie das Edict betreffend Regulirung der gutsherrlich-bäuerlichen Verhältnisse von demselben Tage, wurden die Bestimmungen des Edicts vom 9. October 1807, namentlich in Betreff der Verleihung des erblichen Eigenthums an die Besitzer dienstpflichtiger Grundstücke und Ablösung gutsherrlicher Dienste und Abgaben, sowie in Betreff der Ablösung von Hütungs- und Weide-Berechtigungen und der Theilung gemeinschaftlicher Grundstücke im Einzelnen näher ausgeführt. Durch das erstgedachte Edict ward namentlich auch die unbeschränkte Theilbarkeit des Grundeigenthums gewährleistet, von der im §. 2. des Gesetzes gerühmt wird, daß sie „den sogenannten kleinen Leuten, Käthnern, Büdnern, Häuslern und Tagelöhnern Gelegenheit gebe, ein Eigenthum zu erwerben und zu vermehren.“

§. 38.

Für die Verhältnisse des Bürgerstandes war es von höchster Wichtigkeit, daß bei Einführung der Gewerbe-Steuer, welche durch die erhöhten Bedürfnisse des Staats nothwendig geworden war, zugleich durch das Edict vom 2. November 1810 die Zunft- und exclusiven Gewerbe-Berechtigungen aufgehoben und allgemeine Gewerbefreiheit eingeführt wurde.

Zu den das materielle Recht betreffenden Gesetzen müssen wir endlich noch rechnen das Edict, betreffend die bürgerlichen Verhältnisse der Juden vom 11. März 1812. Durch dasselbe wurde den zu jener Zeit im Staate wohnhaften Juden die Pflicht auferlegt, Familiennamen zu führen, und wurden sie in allen bürgerlichen Verhältnissen den Christen gleichgestellt, während ihnen der Zutritt zu öffentlichen Aemtern versagt blieb. Wie groß die Wohlthat dieses Gesetzes für die Juden war, erkennt man durch Vergleichung desselben mit den frühern gesetzlichen Bestimmungen, namentlich dem Juden-Edict von 1750. Nach letzterm waren die Juden nicht nur vom Erwerb von Grundbesitz ausgeschlossen, sondern sie waren in Bezug auf Verheirathung und Niederlassung den weitgehendsten, zum Theil äußerst erniedrigenden Beschränkungen unterworfen. In manchen Städten durften sie sich gar nicht aufhalten, in andern mußten sie Leibzoll zahlen. Es war überhaupt nur eine bestimmte Anzahl Juden geduldet; als Friedrich II. z. B. im Jahre 1772 Westpreußen erwarb, setzte er sofort fest, wie viel von den dort ansäßigen Juden wohnen bleiben dürften und alle übrigen, deren Zahl man auf 4000 angiebt, wurden ohne Weiteres aus dem Lande gejagt.

§. 39.

Auch in Bezug auf die Organisation der Behörden erfolgten wichtige Aenderungen. Die Verordnung vom 16. December 1808 wegen verbesserter Einrichtung der Polizei-, Provinzial- und Verwaltungs-Behörden und die Verordnung vom 27. October 1810 über die veränderte Verfassung der obersten Staats-Behörden bestimmten den Wirkungskreis des Staatsraths, welcher gänzlich aufhörte, Verwaltungs-Behörde zu sein und dessen Haupt-Function auf die Berathung der ihm Seitens der Regierung überwiesenen Gesetz-Entwürfe beschränkt ward und der einzelnen Ministerien. Zugleich wurden durch diese Verordnungen die gegenseitigen Ressort-

Verhältnisse der Verwaltungs- und Justiz-Behörden anders wie bisher bestimmt; die Provinzial-Verwaltungs-Behörden erhielten statt des bisherigen Namens „Kriegs- und Domainen-Kammern" den Namen Regierungen.

Den Städten ward ihre Gerichtsbarkeit im Jahre 1808 genommen und solche königlichen Gerichten übertragen. Die Aufhebung der Patrimonial-Gerichtsbarkeit ward zwar schon durch eine im Jahre 1808 an den Justiz-Minister Beyme erlassene Cabinets-Ordre für wünschenswerth erklärt, unterblieb jedoch noch.

Die Verfassung der Städte ward neu geordnet durch die bekannte Städte-Ordnung vom 19. November 1808. Die Neuerungen derselben beruhten auf einem doppelten Principe. Es ward nämlich die Aufsicht der Regierungs-Behörden über die städtische Verwaltung verringert und somit die Selbstständigkeit der Städte nach obenhin vermehrt, zugleich aber ward den Bürgern selbst mehr Antheil an Verwaltung der städtischen Angelegenheiten gegeben.

Während früher die Magisträte der Regel nach sich selbst durch Cooptation ergänzten, übertrug die Städte-Ordnung die Wahl der Magistrats-Mitglieder den Stadtverordneten, welche aus der Wahl der Bürgerschaft hervorgingen, und legte die Entscheidung über alle wichtigern städtischen Angelegenheiten in die Hände des Magistrats und der Stadtverordneten.

Eine neue Landgemeinde-Ordnung und neue Regulirung der ländlichen Polizei unter Aufhebung der Polizei-Gewalt der Ritterguts-Besitzer waren von der Gesetzgebung beabsichtigt. Das Gendarmerie-Edict vom 30. Juli 1812 sprach bereits aus, daß an der Spitze der Polizei-Verwaltung jedes Kreises der Landrath oder Kreis-Director stehen sollte, daß sämmtliche Dorfgemeinden selbstständig, daß die Rittergüter mit den Gemeinden vereinigt werden sollten und daß aus frei gewählten Vertretern der Gemeinden die Kreis-Vertretung zu bilden sei. Bekanntlich wurden jedoch diese Bestimmungen des Gendarmerie-Edicts niemals in Ausführung gebracht. —

§. 40.

Die Veränderungen im Militair-Wesen waren höchst durchgreifend und standen in Einklang mit der durch die übrige Gesetzgebung ausgesprochenen Aufhebung der kastenartigen Sonderung der Stände.

Schon durch die Verordnung vom 9. Februar 1813 erfolgte für die Dauer des damals ausbrechenden Kriegs die Aufhebung aller Befreiungen von der Militairpflicht, so daß in dieser Beziehung der Edelmann und Bauer, Städter und Landmann, der Reichste wie der Aermste gleich gestellt wurden. Die Möglichkeit der Stellvertretung beim Militair-Dienst ward zugleich gesetzlich ausgeschlossen. Nach glücklich beendigtem Kriege wurde hiernächst die neue Militair-Verfassung durch die Verordnung vom 3. September 1814 definitiv festgestellt.

Ihre Grundsätze namentlich die Eintheilung der Armee in Linie und Landwehr ersten und zweiten Aufgebots sind bekannt.

Unter den größern Staaten Europa's ist Preußen der erste, welcher in neuerer Zeit seine Armee zu einem wahren Volksheer gemacht hat. Noch ist allerdings seit 1815 keine Gelegenheit gewesen, die Preußische Militair-Organisation der wahrhaft entscheidenden Probe eines großen Krieges zu unterwerfen; wo indessen Preußische Truppen wenn auch nur in kleinern Gefechten Gelegenheit hatten, ins Feuer zu kommen, wie in Schleswig im Jahre 1848 und 1849 im Posenschen und bei dem Badischen Feldzuge im Jahre 1849, haben sie überall die alte Kriegstüchtigkeit im vollen Maaße bewährt. Unser Staat hat durch seine Militair-Organisation den Vortheil erreicht, jedem feindlichen Angriffe ein im Verhältniß zu unserer Bevölkerung außerordentlich großes Heer entgegenzusetzen; zu Eroberungs-Kriegen ist allerdings die Preußische Heeresverfassung durchaus ungeeignet. Dies hat man von Anfang an wohl erkannt. Es war aber auch bei Einführung der neuen Militair-Verfassung die Absicht des wahrhaft frommen und rechtschaffenen Königs Friedrich Wilhelm III., daß der Staat für die Zukunft keine andere als gerechte Vertheidigungskriege führen sollte.

Dieser Absicht entspricht unsere Militair-Verfassung im vollen Maaße. Wenn eine ähnliche Militair-Organisation, wie jetzt in Preußen besteht, auch im übrigen Europa mehr und mehr zur Anwendung kommen sollte, so würde dies gewiß wesentlich dazu beitragen, den Ausbruch von Kriegen zwischen den Nationen Europa's seltener als bisher zu machen.

§. 41.

Auch die Gesetzgebung in Betreff der indirecten und directen Steuern erfuhr eine durchgreifende Reform. In Bezug auf erstere ward das alte Prohibitiv-System aufgegeben und wurden die Zoll-Linien zwischen den einzelnen Provinzen aufgehoben, doch können wir auf die Details dieser Gesetzgebung um so weniger eingehen, da die dauernde Regulirung des Preußischen Finanz- und Steuer-Wesens erst durch die Gesetze vom 30. Mai 1820 erfolgt ist. Hervorheben müssen wir nur noch in Bezug auf die directe Besteuerung, daß durch das Gesetz vom 27. October 1810 (G.-S. S. 25) alle Grundsteuer-Befreiungen aufgehoben wurden.

Das Gesetz verordnet wörtlich:

> „Auf dem kürzesten Wege wird daher auch ein neues Kataster angelegt werden, um die Grundsteuer danach zu bestimmen. Unsere Absicht ist hierbei keinesweges auf eine Vermehrung der bisher aufgekommenen Steuern gerichtet, sondern nur auf eine gleiche und verhältnißmäßige Vertheilung derselben auf alle Grundsteuerpflichtigen. Jedoch sollen alle Exemtionen wegfallen, die weder mit der natürlichen Gerechtigkeit noch mit dem Geist der Verwaltung in benachbarten Staaten länger vereinbar sind. Die bis jetzt von der Grundsteuer befreit gewesenen Grundstücke sollen also ohne Ausnahme damit belegt werden“ ꝛc.

Bekanntlich sind jedoch die Bestimmungen dieses Gesetzes bis jetzt unausgeführt geblieben.

§. 42.

Ueberblickt man diese Gesetzgebung der Jahre 1806—1813 im Zusammenhange, so ist unleugbar, daß dieselbe im Wesentlichen

Alles das in Preußen einführte, was die Französische National-Versammlung in jener berühmten Sitzung vom 5. August 1789 für Frankreich angeordnet hatte. Aber der Erfolg dieser Reformen war in unserm Vaterlande ein durchaus anderer als in Frankreich.

Dort war keine friedliche Durchführung der Reformen möglich, denn der Adel lehnte sich gegen dieselbe offen auf und die Emigranten riefen zuletzt die bewaffnete Einmischung des Auslandes herbei, weniger um den wankenden Thron ihres Königs zu schützen, als um ihre verlorenen Privilegien wieder zu erlangen; auf der andern Seite brannten die Französischen Bauern, kaum aus den Fesseln der Gutsunterthänigkeit erlöst, die Schlösser der Edelleute nieder und bewiesen durch furchtbare Excesse, wie wenig sie für wirkliche Freiheit reif waren.

Auch in Preußen fehlte es nicht an solchen, die mit den Reformen der Gesetzgebung höchst unzufrieden waren. Wir wollen nur an die Versammlung der Märkischen Stände im Jahre 1811 erinnern, in welcher die Regierung einer so heftigen Opposition begegnete, daß der Fürst von Hardenberg sich veranlaßt sah, einen der kühnsten Sprecher der Stände, den Rittergutsbesitzer von Marwitz, auf die Festung zu schicken. Nirgends kam jedoch Seitens der bisher bevorrechteten Stände eine ähnliche Auflehnung gegen die Regierung vor, wie sie Seitens des Französischen Adels durch die Emigration erfolgte; ebensowenig wurden Seitens der freigewordenen Gutsunterthanen in unserm Vaterlande Excesse begangen, wie sie in Frankreich schon im Jahre 1789 so vielfach vorgekommen waren.

§. 43.

Dazu, daß es in unserm Vaterlande gelang, die Reformen in so durchaus legaler und friedlicher Weise einzuführen, haben hauptsächlich wohl zwei Umstände mitgewirkt.

Einmal fühlte sich gerade in der Zeit von 1806—1813 die ganze Nation, so sehr sie auch sonst durch Standesvorurtheile und Verschiedenartigkeit der Interessen getrennt sein mochte, auf's Innigste vereint durch den Haß gegen den gemeinsamen Feind, welcher den Frieden von Tilsit zu einer offenbar vertragswidrigen Plünderung und Bedrückung unseres Vaterlandes gemißbraucht hatte.

Sodann aber — und dies darf man wohl als entscheidend betrachten, — war Friedrich Wilhelm III. ein weit kräftigerer Monarch als Ludwig XVI. Hof, Adel, Geistlichkeit und Beamtenstand waren nicht so demoralisirt, wie in Frankreich, die ganze Nation endlich stand, Dank den Wirkungen der Reformation, auf einer höheren Stufe der geistigen und sittlichen Bildung als in Frankreich.

§. 44.

Die Namen der Männer, welche unter den Auspicien Friedrich Wilhelms III. die so schwierige Reorganisation des Staates leiteten, sind bekannt; es waren, wenn wir von den Urhebern der militairischen Reorganisation, den Generalen von Scharnhorst, von Boyen, u. s. w. absehen, vorzugsweise der Freiherr von Stein, von Schön, Fürst Hardenberg, Beyme.

So groß das Verdienst dieser Männer ist, so darf man über demselben doch nicht das des Königs selbst vergessen. Friedrich Wilhelm III. war durchaus nicht ein Regent, der sich willenlos von seiner Umgebung hätte leiten lassen. Dies bewies er z. B. dadurch, daß er 1809 und 1812 gegen den Willen des Hofes und der Armee an dem Bündniß mit Frankreich festhielt, daß er aber, als er endlich 1813 weniger durch seine eigene Nation und Armee als durch Napoleon selbst zum Kriege gegen Frankreich genöthigt war, diesen Krieg mit Festigkeit bis zum gänzlichen Sturze seines Gegners fortführte. Hätte der König nicht wirklich sich vom Nutzen und der Nothwendigkeit der Reformen überzeugt gehabt, so würde er sich schwerlich durch seine Minister haben bestimmen lassen, sie einzuführen, oder er würde wenigstens nach dem Jahre 1815 den alten Zustand wieder hergestellt haben. Was hätte den König abhalten können, 1815 das Beispiel Friedrichs II. nachzuahmen, der während des siebenjährigen Krieges eine große Anzahl bürgerlicher Officiere in die Armee hatte aufnehmen müssen, diese aber nach dem Frieden mit sehr wenigen Ausnahmen wieder aus der

Armee entfernte, und das ausschließliche Recht des Adels auf Officier-Stellen wiederherstellte!

Gänzlich unrichtig ist es auch, wenn man, wie zuweilen geschieht, fast ausschließlich dem Freiherrn von Stein das Verdienst der Reorganisation des Staats zuschreibt.

Das Edict vom 9. October 1807 war schon im Entwurf fast vollendet, als Stein in das Ministerium trat, die wichtigen Gesetze der Jahre 1810 und 1812 sind lange nach dem Ausscheiden Steins aus dem Preußischen Staatsdienste erlassen.

Wenn man oft behaupten hört, daß Steins Absicht dahin gegangen sei, die Reform der Preußischen Gesetzgebung durch eine freie constitutionelle Verfassung zu krönen, so ist es allerdings richtig, dast er die Absicht hatte, die absolute Macht des Königs und vorzüglich die Allmacht der Büreaukratie zu beschränken, aber diese Beschränkung sollte doch wesentlich nur zum Vortheil der Aristokratie stattfinden, denn Stein war seiner Gesinnung nach von Hause aus Aristokrat und sah das Heil des Vaterlands vor allen Dingen in der Hebung der Aristokratie. Hierüber lassen namentlich die Mittheilungen seines Freundes des spätern Oberpräsidenten von Schön keinen Zweifel. Schon im Jahre 1806 und wiederholt in den spätern Jahren betrieb Stein nach Schön's Mittheilung Nichts mit so großem Eifer, als den Plan, den Geldbedürfnissen des Staats durch Ausgabe einer großen Masse unverzinslichen mit Zwangs-Cours versehenen Papiergeldes abzuhelfen. Es wurde ihm eingewendet, daß in Oestreich das während des Krieges vom Staate ausgegebene Geld auf ein Fünftel seines Nominalwerths herabgesunken sei; er erklärte jedoch gerade dies für einen Vortheil, indem er anführte, „in Oestreich sei das Papiergeld entwerthet, und daher der Werth aller Verkaufsgegenstände namentlich des Getreides, welcher in Papiergeld als dem gesetzlichen Zahlmittel berechnet werde, auf das Vierfache des frühern Preises gestiegen; die Oestreichischen Gutsbesitzer bezögen daher von ihren Gütern jetzt allerdings in dem wohlfeilen Papiergeld drei bis viermal so viel Revenüen als vor dem Kriege und hätten in Folge dessen ihre Schulden während des

Kriegs bezahlen können. Folge der Ausgabe des Papiergeldes sei daher für Oestreich gewesen, daß die Gutsbesitzer sich auf Kosten der städtischen Bevölkerung namentlich der Capitalisten bereichert, und daß nur die letztern von den Nachtheilen des Krieges zu leiden gehabt hätten. Es sei zu wünschen, daß es in Preußen ebenso gemacht werde.“ Ein Staatsmann der derartige Ansichten hat, kann wohl nur zur Partei der äußersten Rechten d. i. zu der Partei gezählt werden, welche man gegenwärtig als Kreuz-Zeitungs-Partei zu bezeichnen pflegt.

Dies darf uns zwar nicht hindern, die Festigkeit und Energie in Steins Charakter namentlich seine bei vielen Gelegenheiten bewiesene Freiheit von Egoismus auf's Höchste anzuerkennen, allein es ist ein Unrecht gegen von Schön, Hardenberg, Beyme, gegen Friedrich Wilhelm III. und vor Allem gegen die geschichtliche Wahrheit, dem Stein allein das Verdienst der Reorganisation des Staats zuzuschreiben und ihm das Project einer wahrhaft constitutionellen Verfassung mit einer Vertretung nicht blos einzelner bevorrechteter Stände, sondern des ganzen Volkes, welches Project er nie gehabt hat und nach seiner ganzen Geistesrichtung nicht haben konnte, unterzuschieben.

Dagegen darf, wenn man einmal über das Verdienst der Urheber jener großen Gesetzgebung urtheilen will, nicht unerwähnt bleiben, daß bei den meisten der von 1806—1813 in Preußen erlassenen Gesetze dem Gesetzgeber offenbar das Muster der gleichzeitig im Königreich Westphalen gegebenen Gesetze vorschwebte. Die Bezugnahme auf letztere ist z. B. im Gendarmerie-Edict vom 30. Juli 1812 und im Gesetze vom 27. October 1810 über Regulirung des Abgaben-Wesens und Aufhebung der Grundsteuer-Befreiungen ausdrücklich ausgesprochen, in andern Gesetzen ist sie zwar nicht ausdrücklich ausgesprochen, aber aus dem Inhalte des Gesetzes ersichtlich.

Es ist eigenthümlich, daß gerade in der Zeit des bittersten und nur zu sehr gerechtfertigten Hasses gegen die Franzosen unser Staat nach dem Muster des von einem Franzosen beherrschten Königreichs

Westphalen seine Gesetzgebung umgestaltete und ist es für die Staatsmänner, welche damals an der Spitze Preußens standen, gewiß im höchsten Grade ruhmvoll, daß sie sich nicht durch nationale Abneigung abhalten lassen, das Neue und Gute vom Feinde des Vaterlandes zu entlehnen. Will man sie deshalb aus einem Uebermaaße nationaler Empfindlichkeit tadeln, so darf man auch die Preußischen Heerführer im Befreiungskriege, namentlich Blücher, Bülow, Gneisenau, nicht ohne Tadel lassen, denn auch diese gingen beim Feinde in die Lehre und wandten die Grundsätze der Strategie, welche sie ihrem großen Gegner dem Kaiser Napoleon abgesehen hatten, zu dessen Verderben an.

§. 45.

Der glückliche Krieg von 1813 bis 1815 gab unserm Staate durch den Wiener Friedens-Schluß sein gegenwärtiges Territorium. Die Verwaltung des Staats wurde im Wesentlichen in den neuerworbenen Provinzen überall nach dem Muster der altländischen Provinzen regulirt.

Durch die Verordnung vom 30. April 1815 ward nämlich der Staat in zehn Provinzen getheilt, deren Zahl später bekanntlich auf 8 herabgesetzt ist, jede Provinz ward in mehrere Regierungs-Bezirke, diese in Kreise getheilt, zu vorgesetzten Verwaltungs-Behörden der Kreise wurden die Landräthe ernannt, als oberste Verwaltungs-Behörden der Regierungs-Bezirke die collegialisch formirten Regierungs-Collegien eingerichtet, welche zwar direct unter dem Ministerio stehn, jedoch in manchen Beziehungen der Aufsicht des Ober-Präsidenten als des obersten Verwaltungsbeamten der Provinz unterworfen sind.

Auch in Bezug auf die Militair-Verfassung erfolgten durch das schon erwähnte Gesetz vom 3. September 1814 gleichförmige Anordnungen für alle Provinzen; ebenso wurden in Bezug auf das Steuerwesen alle Provinzen einander gleich gestellt, mit Ausnahme der Grundsteuer, hinsichtlich deren jede Provinz ihre besondere Verfassung behielt.

Dagegen behielt die Rheinprovinz das zur Zeit der Französischen Herrschaft eingeführte Gerichtsverfahren nebst dem Französischen Civil- und Criminalrecht, ebenso behielten die Provinz Neuvorpommern und der Bezirk des Justiz-Senats Ehrenbreitenstein das dort geltende gemeine Recht. Nur in den übrigen Provinzen ward das Allgemeine Land-Recht mit den bis zum Jahre 1815 vorgenommenen Modificationen nebst der Preußischen Gerichtsverfassung und Gerichtsordnung eingeführt.

§. 46.

Die wichtigste Frage nun in Bezug auf die innere Organisation des Staats, welche sich dem Gesetzgeber schon seit dem Jahre 1815 aufdrängte, war die der Verleihung einer Verfassung.

Nach Außen hin war der König völlig unabhängiger Souverain, denn die seit mehr als einem Jahrhundert illusorische Abhängigkeit vom Deutschen Reiche hatte durch Auflösung desselben im Jahre 1806 auch formell ihre völlige Endschaft erreicht, der Deutsche Bund, welcher an die Stelle des Deutschen Reichs treten sollte, war von Anfang an nur, wie die Wiener Schlußacte sagt, „ein völkerrechtliches Bündniß zwischen den Fürsten und freien Städten Deutschlands, welches Bündniß so wenig wie andere Verträge die Souverainität des Königs beeinträchtigen konnte.

Es entstand nun die Frage, ob der König gegenüber seinen Unterthanen ein völlig absoluter Monarch nach Art des Kaisers von Rußland oder der Orientalischen Herrscher bleiben oder aber ob er selbst seine Machtvollkommenheit durch eine Verfassung beschränken wollte.

Schon in den Gesetzen vom 27. October 1810 und 7. September 1811 war eine zweckmäßig eingerichtete ständische Verfassung verheißen. Demnächst war in der Verordnung vom 22. Mai 1815 ausgesprochen, daß „aus den zu bildenden Provincial-Ständen eine Landes-Repräsentation mit dem Sitze in Berlin gebildet werden sollte.“ Die Wirksamkeit dieser Landes-Repräsentation sollte sich auf die Berathung über alle Gegenstände der Gesetzgebung erstrecken, welche die persönlichen und Eigenthums-Verhältnisse der Staatsbürger mit Einschluß der Besteuerung betreffen.

Im Einklang mit diesem Versprechen hatte Preußen bei Abfassung der Deutschen Bundes-Acte veranlaßt, daß die bekannte Verheißung von Artikel 13. der Bundes-Acte gegeben wurde („In allen Bundes-Staaten wird eine landständische Verfassung stattfinden") und waren längere Zeit hindurch die Bemühungen der Preußischen Regierung dahin gerichtet gewesen, die Verheißung dieses Artikels bestimmter zu fassen und namentlich ein bestimmtes Maaß der Rechte, welche den Ständen jedes Staats zu verleihen seien, festzustellen.

Ueber den Inhalt der zu verleihenden Verfassung entstanden jedoch bekanntlich die erheblichsten Meinungs-Verschiedenheiten in der mit Ausarbeitung derselben beauftragten Commission; die liberalen Mitglieder dieser Commission, namentlich von Humboldt und Beyme, schieden aus ihr aus und es ward demnächst an Stelle der verheißenen Verfassungs-Urkunde das Gesetz vom 5. Juni 1823 über Bildung von Provinzial-Ständen gegeben, worauf in den Jahren 1823 und 1824 durch besonderes Gesetz für jede einzelne Provinz die Zusammensetzung der Provinzial-Stände erfolgte.

Diese Stände bestanden bekanntlich aus Vertretern der Ritterschaft, d. h. der Rittergutsbesitzer, der Städte und des Bauernstandes, sowie in einigen Provinzen noch aus Vertretern des Herrenstandes. Sie hatten nur eine berathende Stimme in Bezug auf die Gesetze, welche die Regierung für gut fand, ihnen vorzulegen, auch durften sie Anträge und Petitionen nur in Betreff solcher Gegenstände abfassen, welche nicht den ganzen Staat sondern nur die specielle Provinz betrafen.

Die Oeffentlichkeit ihrer Berathungen war ausgeschlossen, ihr Zusammentritt erfolgte immer nur in Jahre langen Zwischenräumen; das ganze Institut blieb daher wenigstens bis zur Regierung Friedrich Wilhelms IV. fast ganz bedeutungs- und wirkungslos und fand so wenig im Inlande als im Auslande irgend welche Beachtung. Da nun auch die Presse seit dem Jahre 1819 durch die Censur an einer freimüthigen Besprechung inländischer Angelegenheiten fast ganz verhindert war, war die Entscheidung über alle öffentlichen Angelegenheiten lediglich in den Händen des Königs und seiner Beamten und eine eigentliche Einwirkung der Nation selbst auf Staats-Angelegenheiten fand während der Jahre 1815 bis 1840 gar nicht statt.

§. 47.

Dennoch war diese Zeit für unser Vaterland eine höchst glückliche. Rascher, als seit Jahrhunderten der Fall gewesen war, nahmen Bevölkerung und Wohlstand des Landes zu. Die überwiegende Mehrheit der Nation war zufrieden. Trotz der absoluten Gewalt des Königs herrschte nirgends im Staate Willkühr der Behörden, sondern überall nur das Gesetz. Der Grund für letztere Thatsache lag nicht bloß in der Persönlichkeit des Königs Friedrich Wilhelms III., der mit Ernst und Festigkeit die Behörden überwachte, sondern hauptsächlich in dem Geiste, welcher im Allgemeinen im Beamten-Stande herrschte.

Niemand hat sich hierüber mit mehr Sachkenntniß, Offenheit und Klarheit ausgesprochen, als der berühmte Gans in seinen 1830—1832 erschienenen Beiträgen zur Revision der Preußischen Gesetzgebung, Seite 285 ff.

Gans sagt an der angeführten Stelle wörtlich:

„Die bürgerliche Freiheit im Preußischen Staate liegt in der gesetzlichen Organisation der Verwaltung, in dem, was die Franzosen seit einigen Jahren mit dem Namen Ordre légal bezeichnen und noch vergebens zu erhalten bemüht sind. Die Beamten sind nicht den Verwalteten gegenüber eine Macht und somit ein Anderes, sondern da sie nur Organe des Gesetzes sind und sich als solche bewegen, so stellen sie ebensogut die Verwalteten dar und sind als Repräsentanten derselben zu betrachten. Es ist der große Unterschied des Staatsdienstes in Frankreich und in Preußen, daß in dem ersteren Lande derselbe gleichsam als das Gegengewicht der gesetzlichen Verfassung betrachtet wird, in dem letztern aber fast die Verfassung selbst ausmacht. .... Dagegen ist in Preußen der Beamte Nichts als der Diener und Ausführer des Gesetzes und weil Fürst und Volk im Gesetze zusammentreffen, sowohl der Diener des Fürsten als der Repräsentant des Volks. Dieser Unterschied . . . zeigt sich schon in der Art, wie der Beamten-Stand entsteht.

Bei uns setzt er sich gleichsam auf democratische Weise selbst an, indem der Einzelne in eine allen geöffnete Laufbahn eintritt, und durch Examina sich allmälig ohne eine andere Beförderung als die seines selbstständigen Verdienstes erhebt."

§. 48.

Viele Gründe hatten zusammengewirkt, diese von Gans mit Recht gerühmte eigenthümliche Bildung des Beamten-Standes herbeizuführen. Hauptsächlich aber kommt in Betracht, daß seit der Zeit der Reformation fast im ganzen nördlichen Deutschland die tüchtigsten Männer des Mittelstandes sich Anfangs der Theologie später der Beamten-Laufbahn gewidmet hatten, daß auch für den Adel die Beamten-Laufbahn die größte Anziehung hatte.

Diese Laufbahn war, nachdem die ständischen Versammlungen zur Unbedeutendheit hinabgesunken waren, neben der militairischen Carriere die einzige, welche eine bedeutende Einwirkung auf die öffentlichen Angelegenheiten verschaffte und dadurch die ehrenvollste Stellung im bürgerlichen Leben gewährte. In Preußen kam hinzu, daß seit der Zeit Friedrich Wilhelms I. die Beamten zwar von Oben her mit Strenge überwacht, aber in der Regel nicht nach Gunst, sondern nach ihrer persönlichen Tüchtigkeit oder nach Gründen der Anciennität befördert und zugleich, was jetzt leider nicht mehr der Fall ist, auskömmlich besoldet wurden.

Ob bei den gegenwärtigen Verhältnissen, namentlich wenn man die jetzigen ganz ungenügenden Gehalte der meisten Beamten nicht erheblich erhöht, die Beamten im Ganzen und Großen sich noch lange auf der gegenwärtigen Höhe der Bildung und Tüchtigkeit werden behaupten können, ist eine Frage, die wir gern unerörtert lassen.

§. 49.

Das Verlangen nach einer freiern Verfassung und einer größern Betheiligung der Nation an der Leitung der öffentlichen Angelegenheiten machte sich nun seit 1815 von Jahr zu Jahr mehr geltend. Beim Regierungs-Antritt Friedrich Wilhelms IV. wurde dies Verlangen in der bekannten Adresse der Ostpreußischen Stände offen ausgesprochen. Die größere Preßfreiheit, welche seit 1840 Seitens der Regierung bewilligt wurde, diente nur dazu, das Verlangen nach einer freien Verfassung stärker und allgemeiner zu machen. Nach langen Vorbereitungen erschien endlich das Patent vom 3. Februar 1847 über Bildung des vereinigten Landtags. Derselbe bestand bekanntlich aus einem Herrnhause und einem Hause der Abgeordneten. Beide Häuser waren, abgesehen von den zum Herrnhause gezogenen Königlichen Prinzen, lediglich aus den Mitgliedern der sämmtlichen Provinzial-Stände gebildet.

Der vereinigte Landtag hatte nur eine berathende Stimme, abgesehen von der Bewilligung neuer Steuern, hinsichtlich deren er eine entscheidende Stimme hatte. Sein Zusammentritt sollte immer nur auf specielle Berufung durch die Regierung erfolgen.

Durch Bildung des vereinigten Landtags sollte nun, wie in dem Königlichen Patente gesagt war, das in der Verordnung vom 22. Mai 1815 gegebene Versprechen des Königs in vollem Maaße erfüllt sein. Wirklich war auch, wie wir gesehen haben, in jener Verordnung von 1815 nur von einer aus den Provinzial-Ständen zu bildenden Repräsentativ-Versammlung die Rede, deren Wirksamkeit sich auf die Berathung aller Gesetze über persönliche und Eigenthumsrechte erstrecken sollte. Aber mochte nun das Patent vom 3. Februar 1847 die Verheißungen jener Verordnung erfüllen oder nicht, die Nation im Allgemeinen fand ihre politischen Wünsche durch Bildung des vereinigten Landtags nicht befriedigt.

Dennoch glaubte Niemand schon für die nächsten Jahre politischen Unruhen in unserm Vaterlande entgegensehen zu müssen, aber der unerwartete Ausbruch der Revolution vom 24. Februar 1848 zu Paris hatte die März-Revolution in unserm Vaterlande zur Folge.

Die Ereignisse der Jahre 1848 bis 1850 zu schildern, liegt

außerhalb der Gränzen unserer Aufgabe. Für die politische Entwickelung Preußens Epoche machend war die endliche definitive Feststellung der vom Könige und sämmtlichen Civil-Beamten beschworenen Verfassung vom 31. Januar 1850. Auf dieser Verfassung beruht gegenwärtig das öffentliche Recht des Preußischen Staats.

§. 50.

Die wesentlichen Bestimmungen derselben sind bekannt. Sie sind in der Hauptsache der Belgischen Verfassung des Jahres 1831 nachgebildet und diese stimmt in den meisten Punkten mit der von Ludwig XVIII. im Jahre 1814 verliehenen Charte überein.

Während die executive Gewalt dem Könige allein verblieben ist, ist die gesetzgebende getheilt, zwischen dem Könige und den beiden Kammern, von welchen die erste gegenwärtig, nach Abänderung der ursprünglichen Bestimmungen der Verfassung, hauptsächlich durch Ernennung Seitens des Königs, die zweite durch Wahl Seitens der Nation gebildet wird. Die Ausübung des Wahlrechts zur zweiten Kammer ist nur durch einen geringen Census beschränkt, doch sind sämmtliche Wähler nach Höhe ihres Vermögens in drei Classen getheilt, so daß den begüterten Classen ein überwiegender Einfluß auf den Ausfall der Wahl gesichert ist. — Die Minister sind verantwortlich. Alle Standesvorrechte sind aufgehoben. Die Censur ist abgeschafft. Die freie Verfügung über das Grundeigenthum und die Theilbarkeit desselben sind gewährleistet. Es ist ferner das wichtige Princip der vollen Religions-Freiheit ausgesprochen und festgesetzt, daß der Unterschied der Religion keine Verschiedenheit der bürgerlichen und staatsbürgerlichen Rechte begründen solle, sowie daß die Evangelische und Römisch-Katholische Kirche wie jede andere Religions-Gesellschaft ihre Angelegenheiten selbstständig ordnen sollen.

§. 51.

Vom Deutschen Bunde, dessen Organ, der Bundes-Tag, zur Zeit der Einführung der Verfassung bekanntlich aufgelöst war, ist in der Verfassung nicht die Rede, dagegen ist in Artikel 118. derselben der Fall vorgesehen, daß durch die für den Deutschen Bundesstaat auf Grund des Entwurfs vom 26. Mai 1849 festzustellende Verfassung Aenderungen der Preußischen Verfassung herbeigeführt werden könnten.

Unstreitig ging bei der Beschwörung der Verfassung die Absicht sowohl des Königs als der Kammern dahin, daß die Bestimmungen des Deutschen Bundesrechts namentlich der Wiener Schluß-Acte vom Jahre 1820, — welche sich bekanntlich mit der Existenz wahrhaft constitutioneller Verfassungen in Deutschland nicht vereinigen lassen, — niemals im Widerspruch mit der Verfassung Geltung für das innere Staatsrecht der Preußischen Monarchie haben sollten; der Deutsche Bund ist eben, wie die Wiener Schluß-Acte mit Recht sagt, ein bloß „völkerrechtliches Bündniß der verschiedenen Fürsten und freien Städte Deutschlands," welches Bündniß für das innere Staatsrecht Preußens nicht mehr Geltung haben kann, als anderweite völkerrechtliche Verträge, die Preußen mit andern Staaten z. B. mit Frankreich, Rußland u. s. w. abgeschlossen hat.

§. 52.

Durch die Verfassung ist nun Preußen definitiv in die Reihe der constitutionellen Staaten Europa's eingetreten. Die absolute Machtvollkommenheit des Landesherrn, welche in unserm Vaterlande seit dem dreißigjährigen Kriege factisch bestanden hatte, hat mit dem 31. Januar 1850 aufgehört.

Die überwiegende Mehrheit der Nation ist mit der Umwandlung der absoluten Monarchie in eine constitutionelle einverstanden gewesen. Freilich fehlt es auch jetzt nicht an solchen, welche mit der Verfassung unzufrieden sind. Diese Unzufriedenheit entspringt, wenn man von der jetzt ganz einflußlosen Partei der äußersten Demokratie absieht, welche an Stelle der Monarchie am liebsten eine Republik setzen möchte, aus einem zwiefachen Grunde, nämlich einmal aus Vorliebe für die absolute Monarchie und sodann aus Abneigung gegen die angeblich zu demokratische Zusammensetzung der zweiten Kammer. Die Vorliebe für die Verfassung der absoluten Monarchie ist wenn irgendwo gewiß in Preußen zu erklären, weil unser Vaterland unleugbar durch die unumschränkte Herrschergewalt seiner Fürsten groß geworden ist. Wir theilen diese Vorliebe nicht. Eine gewisse rechtliche Ordnung muß nothwendig das Verhältniß zwischen dem Herrscher und den Unterthanen regeln. Die Staatsverfassung ist eben Nichts anderes, als die gesetzliche Feststellung dieses Verhältnisses. Wenn man in neueren Zeiten es für ein Unglück erklärt hat, daß die Verfassung, ein Stück Papier, gewissermaßen zwischen den König und sein Volk treten sollte, so vergißt man, daß eine schriftliche Festsetzung von gegenseitigen Rechten und Pflichten dem bloßen ungeschriebenen Herkommen oder der bloßen Willkühr unbedingt vorzuziehen ist.

Hat doch nach dem Zeugniß der heiligen Schrift schon Samuel bei Begründung des Königthums der Israeliten die Rechte des Königs und des Volkes in ein Buch geschrieben, welches neben der Bundeslade aufbewahrt wurde, und wurden doch aus diesem Buche die Rechte des Volkes wie des Königs von Zeit zu Zeit öffentlich verlesen. Wenn das graueste Alterthum es somit für erforderlich hielt, die gegenseitigen Rechte des Königs und des Volks durch schriftliche Urkunde festzustellen, wie viel mehr muß uns dies jetzt bei unsern verwickelten Verhältnissen als nothwendig erscheinen und auf welche andere Weise als durch eine schriftliche Verfassung können diese Rechte festgestellt werden! Gewiß nicht ohne Grund ist die öffentliche Meinung in Deutschland, England, Frankreich, Italien, Spanien, fast in ganz Europa beinahe einstimmig in der Vorliebe für die constitutionell-monarchische Regierungs-Form.

Doch es liegt außerhalb unserer Aufgabe, die Vorzüge oder Nachtheile der constitutionellen oder absolut-monarchischen Regierungs-Form zu erörtern. Darüber freilich, daß der persönliche Einfluß des Königs in unserm Vaterlande noch lange Zeit hindurch ein viel größerer sein muß, als solcher z. B. seit einem Jahrhundert in England ist, kann kein Zweifel sein, da schon mit Rücksicht auf die äußern Verhältnisse unseres Vaterlands, welches drei große Militair-Staaten, Rußland, Frankreich und Oestreich zu Nachbarn hat, eine starke Krone für Preußen ein Bedürfniß ist.

Die Zahl derer, welche die bestehende Verfassung aus bloßer

Vorliebe für die absolut=monarchische Regierungs=Form angreifen, ist übrigens bedeutend geringer, als die Zahl derer, die mit der Verfassung bloß um deswillen unzufrieden sind, weil sie eine mehr aristokratische Zusammensetzung der zweiten Kammer wünschen. Aber eine wahrhaft aristokratische Verfassung der zweiten Kammer, etwa nach Art des vereinigten Landtags oder nach dem Muster der Stände des 17. Jahrhunderts, würde mit den jetzigen socialen Zuständen in Widerspruch stehen. Der Bauer, der jetzt in Reichthum und Bildung oft dem Rittergutsbesitzer gleich ist, kann nicht mehr so wie früher in Bezug auf die ständische Vertretung übergangen oder zurückgesetzt werden, überhaupt aber besteht die ehemalige Trennung der Stände, auf welcher die ganze ältere Verfassung beruhte, jetzt nicht mehr, da ja fast die Hälfte der Rittergüter in den Besitz von Bürgerlichen übergegangen ist und fast jeder Unterschied der Bildung zwischen dem sogenannten höhern Bürgerstande und dem Adel aufgehört hat.

Sollte daher überhaupt der Nation selbst wieder eine gesetzlich geordnete Einwirkung auf die öffentlichen Angelegenheiten gegeben werden, so konnte dies den jetzigen socialen Verhältnissen entsprechend nur durch eine Verfassung geschehen, welche wenigstens bei Zusammensetzung der zweiten Kammer die nicht mehr vorhandenen Standes=Unterschiede unberücksichtigt läßt.

§. 53.

In mancher Beziehung enthält übrigens die Verfassung zwar wesentliche Neuerungen des frühern Rechts, aber doch nur solche Neuerungen, auf welche der Entwickelungsgang unserer Gesetzgebung schon während der letzten Jahrzehende hingeführt hatte. So ist es z. B. mit den Bestimmungen der Verfassung über das Verhältniß des Staats zur Evangelischen und Katholischen Kirche und den sonstigen Religions=Gesellschaften.

Seit Anfang des 17. Jahrhunderts hatte es dem Brandenburg=Preußischen Staate mit Recht zum Ruhm gereicht, daß in ihm ein hoher Grad von religiöser Duldung herrschte. Während der Landesherr reformirter Confession war, waren die Unterthanen der überwiegenden Mehrheit nach Lutheraner; sowohl unter der Regierung des großen Kurfürsten als unter der Friedrichs I. und Friedrich Wilhelms I. fanden Tausende von Protestanten, welche ihrer Religion wegen in ihrem Vaterlande verfolgt wurden, namentlich viele Böhmen, Salzburger, die Refugie's aus Frankreich eine Zufluchtsstätte in unserm Vaterlande. Diese Duldung ging jedoch nicht so weit, daß das Recht der Oberaufsicht des Staats über alle kirchliche Angelegenheiten jemals in Frage gestellt wäre.

Dies Recht übte der Staat sowohl in Bezug auf die Katholische als auf die Lutherische und Reformirte Kirche aus, welche letztere beide bekanntlich hauptsächlich durch die Einwirkung des Königs Friedrich Wilhelms III. sich zur Evangelisch-unirten Kirche vereinigten.

Die Gleichstellung der Katholiken und Protestanten war in Preußen soweit durchgeführt, wie kaum in einem andern größern Staate. In gewisser Beziehung war sogar die Katholische Kirche vor der Evangelischen bevorzugt, denn durch die zur Bestätigung der Bulle de salute animarum jedoch, wie im Gesetze ausdrücklich gesagt ist, unbeschadet der Majestäts-Rechte des Königs erlassene Cabinets-Ordre vom 23. August 1821 war der Katholischen Kirche eine außerordentliche große Dotation aus Staatsmitteln ausgesetzt. Diese Dotation übersteigt bedeutend die Summe, welche für die Evangelische Kirche, der doch mehr als zwei Drittel der Staatsbürger angehören, vom Staate verwendet wird. Doch schon unter der Regierung Friedrich Wilhelms III. führte die Festhaltung des Oberaufsichtsrechts des Staats zu dem bekannten Conflicte mit dem Erzbischof von Cöln. Dieser hatte vor seiner Ernennung zum Erzbischof das Versprechen gegeben, die bestehenden Gesetze hinsichtlich der gemischten Ehen zu beobachten, glaubte aber demnächst es seinem Gewissen schuldig zu sein, dieses Versprechen nicht zu halten und gab durch diesen Wortbruch Anlaß zu seiner gefänglichen Einziehung, welche die größte Aufregung in der Rheinprovinz und Westphalen zur Folge hatte. Friedrich Wilhelm IV. fand sich bald nach Antritt der Regierung bewogen, den Erzbischof von Cöln frei zu lassen, den Verkehr der Katholischen Geistlichkeit mit dem Papste vollkommen freizugeben und überhaupt der Katholischen Kirche schon vor Einführung der Verfassung volle Selbstständigkeit zu gewähren. Seitdem dies geschehen ist, sind alle Conflicte mit der Katholischen Geistlichkeit vermieden, ohne daß der Staat von seinen wesentlichen Rechten irgend etwas eingebüßt hätte. In der Evangelischen Kirche hatte die Einführung der Union und der neuen Liturgie die Bildung sogenannter altlutherischer Gemeinden zur Folge gehabt. Vergeblich hatte man in Aufrechterhaltung der frühern strengen Grundsätze über das jus circa sacra des Staats unter der Regierung Friedrich Wilhelms III. gesucht durch Polizei-Maßregeln den altlutherischen Cultus gänzlich zu unterdrücken. Erst die Regierung Friedrich Wilhelms IV. gewährte den alt-lutherischen Gemeinden volle Religionsfreiheit. Auch den seit dem Jahre 1844 entstehenden Deutsch-Katholischen und den sogenannten freien Gemeinden ward freie Religions-Uebung gestattet, so daß die Principien des Artikels 12. der Verfassung im Wesentlichen schon vor Erlaß der Verfassung zur Anwendung gebracht waren.

Was die Aufhebung der Censur betrifft, so war dieselbe allerdings erst im Jahre 1848 erfolgt, indessen war bereits seit 1840 die Strenge der Censur wesentlich gemildert und war die gänzliche Aufhebung derselben seit Jahren bekanntlich nur durch Rücksicht auf die mit Oestreich geschlossenen Verträge verschoben worden.

§. 54.

Werfen wir unsern Blick von der Staatsverfassung auf das Gebiet des eigentlichen Civilrechts, so finden wir bereits im Jahre 1815 in unserm Staate eine dreifache Gesetzgebung in Geltung, nämlich in der Rheinprovinz den code Napoléon, in der Provinz Neu-Vorpommern und dem Bezirke des Justiz-Senats Ehrenbreitenstein das Römische Recht, in sämmtlichen übrigen Provinzen aber das Allgemeine Land-Recht. Die Abfassung eines einheitlichen Gesetzbuchs für den ganzen Staat ward vom Gesetzgeber beabsichtigt, es ward sogar durch Cabinets-Ordre vom 9. Februar 1832 ein besonderes Gesetzgebungs-Ministerium gebildet, um eine solche herbeizuführen; es ist jedoch bekannt, daß dieses Ministerium, obwohl es bis zum Jahre 1848 bestand, seiner Aufgabe nicht genügt hat. Wesentlich Schuld daran, daß ein neues Gesetzbuch nicht zu Stande kam, war die Vorliebe, mit der man lange Zeit das Provinzial-Recht behandelte.

Sieht man von dem Gebiete des ehelichen Güterrechts ab, so sind jetzt die provinziellen Rechts-Verschiedenheiten materiell nur noch von geringer Bedeutung. Die Bestimmungen, welche zur Zeit der Abfassung des Land-Rechts vorzugsweise zur Rechts-Sphäre der Provinzial-Rechte gehört und wegen deren hauptsächlich die Verfasser des Land-Rechts die Beibehaltung der Provinzial-Rechte für nöthig gehalten hatten, waren die Vorschriften über die gutsherrlich-bäuerlichen Verhältnisse gewesen. In Bezug auf diese aber sind alle provinziellen Verschiedenheiten durch die Gesetzgebung der Jahre 1806—1813 beseitigt.

Dennoch wurde namentlich unter Leitung des Ministers von Kamptz auf die Sammlung und Zusammenstellung der Provinzial-Rechte soviel Arbeit verwendet, daß darüber die Abfassung eines allgemeinen Gesetzbuchs gänzlich versäumt wurde.

Die einzige erhebliche Abänderung des Civil-Rechts, welche wir dem Ministerio für Gesetzgebung verdanken, ist die Allgemeine Deutsche Wechsel-Ordnung. Der Entwurf derselben stammt aus diesem Ministerio, dieser Entwurf erhielt demnächst in einer Berathung von Rechtsverständigen der verschiedenen Deutschen Staaten im Jahre 1847 zu Leipzig diejenige Fassung, in welcher die Wechsel-Ordnung im Jahre 1849 in Folge Beschlusses der National-Versammlung zu Frankfurt am Main als Gesetz für ganz Deutschland publicirt wurde. Der Haupt-Unterschied derselben von den betreffenden Vorschriften des Land-Rechts besteht bekanntlich darin, daß sie die Wechselfähigkeit mit geringen Ausnahmen auf alle handlungsfähigen Personen ausdehnt, während das Allgemeine Land-Recht dieselbe fast bloß auf Kaufleute und Fabrikanten beschränkt hatte. Man ist gegenwärtig wohl fast allgemein darin einig, daß diese

Ausdehnung der Wechselfähigkeit den heutigen Verkehrs-Verhältnissen entspricht und in hohem Grade wohlthätig gewirkt hat.

§. 55.

Während so das Civil-Recht im Ganzen und Großen unverändert blieb, fehlte es doch nicht an einer großen Masse specieller Gesetze, die jedoch an Wichtigkeit den großen Gesetzen der Jahre 1806—1813 weit nachstehn und welche die wesentlichsten Grundzüge jener Gesetze namentlich die persönliche Freiheit aller Einwohner des Staats und die Freizügigkeit unverändert ließen.

In näherer Ausführung der Grundsätze des Edicts vom 14. September 1811 erging die Gemeinheits-Theilungs-Ordnung vom 7. Juni 1821.

Die Leitung der Gemeinheits-Theilungen und Dienstablösungen ward einer durch Verordnung vom 20. Juni 1817 neugebildeten Behörde, den General-Commissionen, anvertraut.

Die Gemeinheits-Theilungen haben allerdings momentan den Interessenten große Kosten verursacht und oft dieselben zu gänzlicher Umänderung ihrer Wirthschaftsmethode genöthigt, aber diese Nachtheile sind, wie jetzt allgemein anerkannt wird, nicht zu vergleichen mit dem Vortheil, der darin liegt, daß es durch diese Separationen möglich ward, große Strecken schlecht benutzter Weiden in Ackerland zu verwandeln oder doch besser wie bisher zu nutzen.

Schon Friedrich II. hatte übrigens durch viele Verordnungen auf die Theilung der seit den ältesten Zeiten in unserm Vaterlande in großer Masse bestehenden Gemeinde-Wiesen und Hütungsflächen hinzuwirken gesucht, doch erst seit 1815 sind derartige Theilungen in unserm Vaterlande allgemeiner durchgeführt worden.

Die Ablösung der gutsherrlich-bäuerlichen Dienste und Abgaben schritt indessen nur langsam fort, erst die Gesetze vom 2. März 1850 über Ablösung der gutsherrlich-bäuerlichen Dienste und Abgaben und Bildung von Renten-Banken, — deren Bestimmungen im Detail zu erörtern außerhalb der Gränzen unserer Aufgabe liegt, — haben eine raschere Ablösung dieser Abgaben zur Folge gehabt.

Die Gewerbefreiheit blieb zwar in den Landestheilen bestehen, in denen sie durch das Edict von 1810 oder, wie in der Rheinprovinz und einem Theile der Provinz Sachsen, durch die ausländische Gesetzgebung eingeführt war, ward jedoch da, wo sie noch nicht bestand, wie namentlich in den vom Königreich Sachsen abgetretenen Landestheilen und der Provinz Neu-Vorpommern, erst durch die Gewerbe-Ordnung vom 17. Januar 1845 eingeführt. Später ist sie bekanntlich nicht unwesentlich beschränkt durch die Gewerbe-Ordnung vom 8. Februar 1849, welche für den handwerksmäßigen Gewerbebetrieb die Nothwendigkeit der Meister- und Gesellen-Prüfungen wieder einführte.

In Bezug auf die Verpflichtung der Ortsbehörden zur Aufnahme neuanziehender Personen erging die Verordnung vom 31. December 1842, Inhalts deren kein Ort der Aufnahme eines arbeitsfähigen und bisher unbescholtenen Inländers sich weigern darf, so daß also das Princip der Freizügigkeit aufrecht erhalten wurde. Erst nach Verleihung der Verfassung ist dies Princip bekanntlich dadurch verletzt, daß den Städten das Recht gegeben ist, die Aufnahme neuanziehender Personen von Erlegung eines Einzugsgeldes abhängig zu machen.

Die Zunahme des Reichthums und der Industrie seit Herstellung des Friedens im Jahre 1815 zeigte sich namentlich auch im Entstehen von Actien-Gesellschaften, welche noch zur Zeit der Abfassung des Land-Rechts in unserm Vaterlande kaum den Namen nach bekannt gewesen waren. Durch das Gesetz vom 9. November 1843 wurden die Rechtsverhältnisse dieser Gesellschaften geregelt, indem namentlich ihre Begründung von der Erlaubniß des Landesherrn abhängig gemacht und ihr ganzer Geschäftsbetrieb der Controlle der Regierung unterworfen ward. — Vermittelst der Actien-Gesellschaften ist es möglich geworden, daß auch solche Unternehmungen, welche für die Geldkräfte eines Einzelnen zu groß waren, von der Privat-Industrie ausgeführt werden konnten. Es zeigte sich dies namentlich bei den Eisenbahnen, welche seit den letzten Jahren der Regierung Friedrich Wilhelm III. in unserm Vaterlande angelegt wurden und namentlich im Anfange fast alle ohne Unterstützung des Staats durch Actien-Gesellschaft gebaut wurden.

§. 56.

Die Armenpflege ward für den ganzen Umfang des Staats neu geordnet durch das Gesetz vom 31. December 1842. Die allerdings jetzt sehr modificirte Grundlage unserer ganzen heutigen Armengesetzgebung bilden die bereits in §. 16. von uns erwähnten Bestimmungen des Armen-Edicts von 1715. Das Allgemeine Land-Recht stellte in §. 1. Theil II. Tit. 19. das Princip auf:

„Dem Staate kommt es zu, für die Ernährung und Verpflegung derjenigen Bürger zu sorgen, die sich ihren Unterhalt nicht selbst verschaffen und denselben auch von andern Privatpersonen, welche nach besondern Gesetzen dazu verpflichtet sind, nicht erhalten können."

Jedoch übertrug das Land-Recht die unmittelbare Ausübung der Armenpflege, ganz wie das Gesetz von 1715, den einzelnen Stadt- und Dorfgemeinden und ließ nur subsidiarisch die Verpflichtung des Staats eintreten.

Behufs Bestreitung der Kosten der Armenpflege, soweit solche nicht aus den Revenüen des Gemeinde-Vermögens sollten gedeckt werden können, wies das Allgemeine Land-Recht den Gemeinden den Ertrag der Collecten an, hob jedoch die Bestimmung des Edicts von 1715 auf, wonach jedermann verpflichtet gewesen war, und erforderlichen Falls zwangsweise hätte angehalten werden können, bei dieser Collecte einen entsprechenden Beitrag zu geben. Für den Fall, daß auch der Ertrag dieser Collecten nicht ausreichend sein sollte, gestattete das Land-Recht den Gemeinden, mit Genehmigung der Regierungsbehörden „die Vergnügungen der wohlhabenden Einwohner mit einer mäßigen Steuer zu belegen."

Das Gesetz vom 31. December 1842 ordnete nun im Anschlusse an die Bestimmungen des Allgemeinen Land-Rechts an, daß den einzelnen Gemeinden resp. den selbstständigen Rittergütern die Pflege ihrer Armen obliege und daß falls eine Gemeinde oder ein Rittergut nicht im Stande sei, dieser Pflicht zu genügen oder falls sich

Arme finden sollten, die in keinem bestimmten Orte heimathsberechtigt seien, der Land-Armen-Verband subsidiarisch zur Unterstützung der Armen verpflichtet sein solle.

Der Umfang der einzelnen Land-Armen-Verbände fällt meistens mit denen der einzelnen Provinzen zusammen. In Bezug auf die Frage, ob einer bestimmten Person Armen-Unterstützung zu gewähren sei, und in Bezug auf die Höhe der zu gewährenden Unterstützung ist die Competenz der Gerichte vollständig ausgeschlossen und steht den Personen, welche sich über nicht genügende Armen-Unterstützung beklagen wollen, nur die Beschwerde bei den Verwaltungs-Behörden frei.

Der Hauptunterschied dieses Gesetzes von dem Armen-Edict von 1715 dürfte der sein, daß letzteres Edict eine strenge Ueberwachung der mit der Armenpflege beauftragten Behörden anordnete und sogar eine zwiefache Controlle durch die Verwaltungs-Behörden und die Geistlichkeit vorschrieb, daß dasselbe ferner den nachlässigen Ortsbehörden strenge Strafen androhte, während so wenig diese Controlle als die Strafandrohung in dem Gesetze vom 31. December 1842 beibehalten sind. Wir müssen offen gestehen, daß wir namentlich den Hinwegfall der im Edict von 1715 angeordneten Controlle der Armenpflege für einen wesentlichen Rückschritt halten. Wäre eine solche Controlle beibehalten worden, so würden Uebelstände, wie z. B. die Hungersnoth und der Hungertyphus in den Schlesischen Kreisen Rybnik und Pleß im Jahre 1847, der Nothstand in Ostpreußen im Jahre 1845, nicht möglich gewesen sein.

Daß unsere jetzige Armenpflege sehr viel zu wünschen übrig läßt, wird jedermann zugeben, der sich auch nur einigermaßen mit der ländlichen Armenpflege der östlichen Provinzen bekannt gemacht hat.

Selbst in den wohlhabendsten Gegenden und in der Nähe großer Städte pflegen noch jetzt die Bettler aus den Dörfern schaarenweise umherzuziehen, weil sie in ihren Heimathsorten nicht soviel Unterstützung erhalten, um davon leben zu können. Die Tendenz der meisten Orts-Schulzen ist lediglich dahin gerichtet, die Armen-Pflege so billig wie möglich zu haben; gegen diese Rücksicht treten alle andern Erwägungen zurück. Eine Besserung in dieser Beziehung wird man nur erwarten können, wenn nach dem Muster der beiden westlichen Provinzen auch im übrigen Staate eine Gemeinde-Ordnung eingeführt würde, welche durch Vereinigung mehrerer Gemeinde-Bezirke die Nachtheile des zu geringen Umfangs der einzelnen Gemeinden aufheben würde. Unsere jetzigen Landgemeinden sind größtentheils von so geringem Umfange, daß sie die Elemente zu einer gedeihlichen Polizei-Verwaltung und Armenpflege nicht darbieten. Außerdem ist im Gesetze nicht bestimmt, wann eine Gemeinde für so unvermögend zu erachten sei, daß der Landarmen-Verband subsidiarisch die Armenpflege zu übernehmen habe; hiervon ist die Folge, daß sehr häufig Gemeinden sich unter dem Vorwand des Unvermögens weigern, ausreichende Armen-Unterstützung zu geben, während doch der Landarmen-Verband sich nicht veranlaßt findet, für die Gemeinden subsidiarisch einzutreten. Wäre festgesetzt, daß jede Gemeinde, die z. B. die Hälfte des Betrages ihrer Staats-Abgaben auf Armenpflege verwendet, befugt sei, im Falle des Mehrbedarfs die Unterstützung des Landarmen-Verbandes in Anspruch zu nehmen, so würde dem so eben erwähnten Uebelstande vorgebeugt sein. Hoffen wir, daß die Reform der Gemeinde- und Kreis-Ordnung der östlichen Provinzen uns auch eine Reform unserer Armen-Gesetzgebung bringen wird!

§. 57.

Im Gebiete des materiellen Criminalrechts erreichte unser Staat durch das Strafgesetzbuch vom 14. April 1851 die Einheit des Rechts, welche uns auf dem Gebiete des Civilrechts noch fehlt.

Das Strafgesetzbuch ist ausgearbeitet weniger mit Benutzung der von dem Ministerio für Gesetzgebung seit einem Vierteljahrhundert aufgehäuften Vorarbeiten als auf Grund des code pénal, dessen Strafbestimmungen in unserm Strafgesetzbuch jedoch wesentlich gemildert sind. Die Prügelstrafe des Allgemeinen Land-Rechts war bereits im Jahre 1848 aufgehoben, das Strafgesetzbuch hat nun auch gesetzlich die bereits seit Jahren nicht mehr vollstreckten geschärften Todesarten aufgehoben, so daß außer der einfachen Todesstrafe, welche nur für das Verbrechen des Mordes oder Hoch= und Landes=Verraths beibehalten ist, das Gesetz nur Freiheits= und Geld=Strafen kennt, welche in gewissen Fällen auch den Verlust der bürgerlichen Ehre zur Folge haben.

Einzelne Bestimmungen des Strafgesetzbuchs sind wegen ihrer zu großen Härte in den nächsten Jahren nach dem Erscheinen desselben abgeändert.

Im Ganzen und Großen ist demselben jedoch sowohl in materieller als in formeller Beziehung der Beifall der öffentlichen Meinung zu Theil geworden.

§. 58.

Erheblicher als die materiellen Rechts=Aenderungen waren die im Gebiete des Gerichts=Verfahrens und der Gerichts=Verfassung seit dem Jahre 1815 vorgenommenen Aenderungen.

Das auf der Allgemeinen Gerichts=Ordnung und der Criminal=Ordnung beruhende Gerichts=Verfahren der alten Provinzen bildete den entschiedensten Gegensatz zu dem zur Zeit der Französischen Herrschaft eingeführten Gerichtsverfahren der Rheinprovinz. Anfangs beabsichtigte man nun, das Gerichtsverfahren der alten Provinzen auch in der Rheinprovinz einzuführen. Dem Berichte des Ministers Beyme dankte man jedoch die vorläufige Beibehaltung des Rheinischen Gerichtsverfahrens. Die Vorzüge desselben namentlich in Bezug auf rasche und gründliche Entscheidung der Civilprozesse machten sich mehr und mehr geltend, so daß man durch die Gesetze vom 1. Juni 1833, 14. December 1833, durch die beiden Verordnungen vom 4. März 1834 und die Verordnung vom 21. Juli 1846 im Civil=Prozeß=Verfahren die wesentlichen Principien der Allgemeinen Gerichts=Ordnung aufhob und durch Bestimmungen ersetzte, welche in der Hauptsache dem Französischen Rechte entlehnt waren. Die Gerichts=Verfassung selbst blieb bei diesen Reformen des Prozesses unverändert bis zum Gesetze vom 2. Januar 1849, welches den eximirten Gerichtsstand aufhob und an Stelle der Patrimonial Gerichte Königliche Gerichte einsetzte.

In Bezug auf den Criminal=Prozeß erfolgte eine vollständige

Reform des altländischen Verfahrens durch die zunächst nur für Berlin erlassene Verordnung vom 17. Juli 1846 und das Gesetz vom 3. Januar 1849, durch welche ein auf das Anklage-Princip und auf Oeffentlichkeit und Mündlichkeit der Schluß-Verhandlung, sowie auf Zuziehung von Geschwornen Behufs Entscheidung der Thatfrage bei Verbrechen gegründeter Strafprozeß eingeführt ward, der im Wesentlichen dem Französischen Strafverfahren nachgebildet ist.

§. 59.

Das Französische Strafverfahren war für unser Vaterland insofern kein neues, als es schon zu Anfang dieses Jahrhunderts in der Rheinprovinz eingeführt war und sich dort längst die allgemeine Anerkennung erworben hatte. Wenn man häufig behaupten hört, daß unser jetziges mündliches und öffentliches Strafverfahren und namentlich das Schwurgerichts Verfahren eine Rückkehr zum alt-germanischen Strafverfahren enthalte, welches letztere seit dem fünfzehnten Jahrhundert in unserm Vaterlande durch den aus dem Kanonischen Recht entlehnten Inquisitions-Prozeß verdrängt worden sei, so ist diese Behauptung nur in sehr beschränkter Weise richtig. Unser heutiges Strafverfahren hat zunächst bei allen Verbrechen und den meisten Vergehen eine schriftliche Voruntersuchung und demnächst auf Grund einer schriftlichen Anklage eine mündliche Verhandlung, in welcher der Richter oder Geschworene auf Grund der erfolgten Beweisaufnahme nach seiner aus dem Inbegriff der Verhandlung geschöpften Ueberzeugung über Schuld oder Unschuld des Angeklagten entscheidet. Das alt-germanische Prozeß-Verfahren dagegen kannte keine geordnete Vor-Untersuchung und die Entscheidung erfolgte der Regel nach nicht in Gemäßheit der durch die Beweisaufnahme entstandenen Ueberzeugung des Richters oder der Schöffen, sondern sie erfolgte, wenn es sich um eine Anklage gegen freie Personen handelte, auf Grund des Resultats, welches das Gottes-Urtheil, der gerichtliche Zweikampf oder der Eidschwur des Angeklagten und seiner Eidhelfer ergab, bei einer Anklage gegen Leibeigene war schon im ältesten Deutschen Gerichtsverfahren neben dem Gottesurtheile die Tortur des Angeklagten in Gebrauch, um dem

Richter die Grundlage zur Entscheidung der Schuldfrage zu verschaffen.

Wenn somit aber auch unser jetziges Strafverfahren von dem alt-germanischen Strafverfahren durchaus verschieden ist und als ein früher unserm Vaterlande unbekanntes angesehen werden muß, so ist dasselbe doch, abgesehen von den mehr als 50jährigen Erfahrungen der Rheinprovinz, empfohlen durch das Beispiel der Rechtspflege Englands und Frankreichs. Was die in den östlichen Provinzen seit dem Jahre 1849 gemachten Erfahrungen betrifft, so ist man unter den Juristen darüber einig, daß unser jetziges mündliches Strafverfahren wenigstens dieselbe Garantie einer gründlichen materiell gerechten Entscheidung als das frühere Verfahren darbietet und dabei eine weit raschere Erledigung der Untersuchungen als früher möglich war, zur Folge hat. Ueber die Vortheile oder Nachtheile der Zuziehung von Geschwornen sind allerdings die Ansichten des juristischen Publikums noch gegenwärtig sehr getheilt.

§. 59.

Während so Organisation und Verfahren der Justizbehörden durchgreifend geändert wurden, blieb die Organisation der Verwaltungsbehörden seit dem Jahre 1817 im Wesentlichen unverändert. Die Funktionen des Ober-Präsidenten, der Regierungen und Landräthe blieben so wie sie im Jahre 1815 bestimmt waren. Die Städte-Ordnung vom 19. November 1808 blieb in den Provinzen in Kraft, in welchen sie eingeführt war, in den Städten eines Theils der neu-erworbenen Provinzen ward die revidirte Städte-Ordnung vom 17. März 1831 eingeführt, welche in den Hauptgrundzügen mit der erstern übereinstimmt.

Dagegen blieb die Landgemeinde-Ordnung der alten Provinzen unverändert, es blieben die gutsherrliche Polizei-Gewalt und die Ober-Aufsicht des Gutsherrn über die Landgemeinden in Kraft. Der Schulze wird noch jetzt wie vor 1806 der Regel nach vom Gutsherrn ernannt, nur braucht er dem Gutsherrn nicht mehr, wie bis zum Edict vom 9. October 1807 geschah, eidlich Gehorsam zu geloben, sondern es genügt ein Versprechen des Gehorsams durch Handschlag an Eidesstatt.

Hierdurch ist in der Landgemeinde-Verfassung die erheblichste Differenz zwischen den sechs östlichen und den beiden westlichen Provinzen, Rheinprovinz und Westphalen, begründet.

In letztern Provinzen ist die gutsherrliche Polizei-Gewalt längst aufgehoben, die einzelnen Landgemeinden sind, soweit sie zu klein sind, um für sich allein ein tüchtiges communales Leben haben zu können, zugleich mit den Rittergütern zu Aemtern oder sogenannten Sammtgemeinden und Bürgermeistereien unter dem Vorsitz eines Amtmanns vereinigt. Diese ihrer wesentlichen Grundlage nach bereits durch die Französische und Westphälische Fremdherrschaft eingeführte Landgemeinde-Verfassung der beiden westlichen Provinzen ward näher ausgebildet unter Verleihung einer größern Selbstständigkeit an die Gemeinden und Aemter durch die Gesetze vom 31. October 1841 und 23. Juli 1845, deren wesentliche materielle Bestimmungen bekanntlich noch jetzt Geltung haben.

Die in den sechs östlichen Provinzen noch bestehende Landgemeinde-Verfassung ist dagegen in offenbarem Widerspruch mit den jetzigen socialen und politischen Verhältnissen.

Gegenwärtig, nachdem die Gutsunterthänigkeit aufgehoben, der Besitz der Rittergüter jedem Staatsbürger ohne Unterschied gestattet und endlich noch die Patrimonialgerichtsbarkeit beseitigt ist, auch die gutsherrlich-bäuerlichen Dienste fast alle abgelöst sind, und der Bauernstand in den letzten Jahrzehenden mehr wie irgend ein anderer Stand an Reichthum und Selbstbewußtsein gewonnen hat, existirt zwischen Ritterguts-Besitzern und Bauern nicht mehr der Unterschied der socialen Stellung und Bildung, der bis 1806 zwischen dem adlichen Ritterguts-Besitzer und dem Cantonpflichtigen Gutsunterthanen bestanden hatte. Es ist daher offenbar unzeitgemäß, noch jetzt jedem Ritterguts-Besitzer ohne Unterschied die obrigkeitliche Gewalt über eine Landgemeinde anzuvertrauen. Eine Reform unserer Landgemeinde-Verfassung, welche in richtiger Erkennung der Verhältnisse schon durch das Gendarmerie-Edict vom 30. Juli 1812 beabsichtigt war, erscheint daher mehr und mehr als nothwendig. Freilich dürfte eine solche Reform nicht darin bestehen können, daß man jede Landgemeinde ohne Weiteres für selbstständig erklärte, denn die wenigsten unserer Landgemeinden haben einen solchen Umfang und namentlich eine hinlängliche Anzahl von gebildeten und wohlhabenden Gemeinde-Gliedern, daß in ihnen ein selbstständiges communales Leben mit eigener Polizei-Verwaltung und eigener Armenpflege auf die Dauer in befriedigender Weise stattfinden könnte. Sowie zu einem gedeihlichen Staats-Leben ein gewisser Umfang des Territoriums des Staats nothwendig ist, so ist auch zu einem selbstständigen communalen Leben ein gewisser Umfang der Commune nothwendig; unmöglich wird man jeden Weiler, jede abgesondert liegende Colonie zu einer selbstständigen Commune machen können, ohne namentlich in Bezug auf Armenpflege und Polizei-Verwaltung Nachtheile herbeizuführen, welche weit größer sein würden, als die Uebelstände, welche mit der jetzigen Unterordnung der Landgemeinden unter die obrigkeitliche Gewalt der Rittergutsbesitzer verbunden sind. Doch alle derartige Nachtheile würden sich vermeiden lassen, wenn man in den sechs östlichen Provinzen einfach die durch die vieljährige Erfahrung erprobte Landgemeinde-Ordnung einer der beiden westlichen Provinzen einführen wollte, in welchen — wie bereits angeführt, — der Nachtheil des zu geringen Umfangs der Gemeinde-Bezirke durch die Vereinigung mehrerer Gemeinden oder Gutsbezirke zu einem Amte oder Bürgermeisterei vermieden ist. —

§. 60.

Werfen wir schließlich noch einen Blick auf die Thätigkeit unserer Gesetzgebung in Bezug auf Steuern und Abgaben, sowie die Finanz-Verhältnisse während der Zeit von 1815 bis 1850.

Die Finanzlage des Staates war unmittelbar nach dem Abschluß des Friedens im Jahre 1815 eine sehr bedrängte. Der Staat bedurfte namentlich für militairische Zwecke auch während des Friedens bedeutender Geldsummen. Dazu kamen die Ausgaben zur Verzinsung der durch den Krieg entstandenen sehr erheblichen Staatsschuld. Nach dem siebenjährigen Kriege war die Entstehung einer Staatsschuld dadurch vermieden, daß Friedrich II. das während des Kriegs geprägte nicht vollwichtige Geld einfach außer Cours setzte. Aehnlich war Oestreich nach dem Jahre 1809 in Bezug auf sein Staats-Papier-Geld verfahren. Der König Friedrich Wilhelm III. vermied dagegen in Folge seiner strengen Rechtlichkeit jede Maßregel, welche man als einen mehr oder weniger verdeckten Staats-Bankerott hätte bezeichnen können, war aber eben dadurch gezwungen, unser Vaterland mit einer Staatsschuld von mehr als 200 Millionen Thalern zu belasten. Im Verhältnisse zu den Schulden der meisten anderen Staaten Europa's, namentlich Englands, Frankreichs, Rußlands mag diese Schuld freilich als klein erscheinen, für die Kräfte unseres Staats jedoch ist sie immerhin recht bedeutend. Das gesammte Abgaben-Wesen des Staats ward nun geregelt durch das Zollgesetz und die Zoll-Ordnung vom 26. Mai 1818, das Gesetz über die Getränke-Steuern und die Steuer vom inländischen Taback vom 8. Februar 1819, ferner das Gesetz über Einrichtung des Abgaben-Wesens vom 30. Mai 1820, sowie die Klassensteuer und Gewerbesteuer von demselben Tage. Wir können ohne auf das Detail dieser Gesetze einzugehen nur die Hauptgrundzüge derselben hervorheben.

Das Zollgesetz hob sämmtliche Binnenzölle im Innern des Staats auf, beseitigte alle Ausfuhr-Verbote und huldigte bei Festsetzung der Einfuhr-Zölle im Allgemeinen den Principien des Freihandels, indem die Zölle hauptsächlich als bloße Finanz-Zölle mit Rücksicht auf die dem Staate zu beschaffende Einnahme und nur ausnahmsweise als Schutzzölle zur Begünstigung der inländischen Industrie festgesetzt wurden.

Der Abschluß der Zollvereins-Verträge, welcher gegenwärtig mit Ausnahme Ostreichs fast ganz Deutschland zu einem einzigen Zoll-System vereinigt hat, ist nur durch das Preußische Zollgesetz vom 26. Mai 1818 möglich geworden.

So außerordentlich groß aber auch die Vortheile sind, welche der Zollverein für Preußen und ganz Deutschland zur Folge gehabt hat, so darf man doch auch den Nachtheil nicht unbeachtet lassen, der für Preußen darin liegt, daß der Zoll-Verein in seiner jetzigen Verfassung jede Aenderung der Zollgesetzgebung unseres Staats von der Einigung fast sämmtlicher Zollvereins-Regierungen abhängig macht und somit jede Reform unserer Zollgesetzgebung auf's Aeußerste erschwert.

§. 61.

Von den directen Steuern können wir hier blos die Grundsteuer in Betracht ziehen. Diese ließ das Gesetz vom 30. Mai 1820 genau in der Art bestehn, wie sie zu jener Zeit bestand, so daß nicht bloß jede Provinz ihre besondere Grundsteuer-Verfassung hat, sondern auch oft in den verschiedenen Landestheilen derselben Provinz ganz verschiedenartige Verfassungen der Grundsteuer bestehen.

In der Rheinprovinz, Westphalen und demjenigen Theile der Provinz Sachsen, der früher zum Königreich Westphalen gehört hat, besteht in Bezug auf die Besteuerung kein Unterschied zwischen städtischem und ländlichem Grundbesitz, zwischen Rittergütern und Bauergütern. In der Mehrzahl der andern Provinzen dagegen sind die Rittergüter bedeutend geringer als die Bauergüter besteuert, indem z. B. in der Mark und Pommern die Rittergüter bloß Lehnpferdegelder statt der Grundsteuer entrichten; die Städte der Provinzen östlich der Elbe entrichten statt der Grundsteuer bloß die Serris-Abgabe, welche so gering ist, daß sie durchaus nicht als Aequivalent der Grundsteuer angesehen werden kann.

Diese Ungleichförmigkeit der Besteuerung hat nicht nur seit Jahrzehnden zu gegenseitigen Beschwerden der einzelnen Provinzen und der verschiedenen Stände gegen einander Anlaß gegeben, sondern sie hat auch den großen Nachtheil für den Staat herbeigeführt, daß die Grundsteuer stationär geblieben ist und jetzt dem Staate nicht mehr einträgt als sie schon im Jahre 1815 eintrug.

Dieser Nachtheil ist von der größten Bedeutung für die Finanz-Verhältnisse des Staats. Wäre im Jahre 1815 die Grundsteuer z. B. auf 5 Procent des Rein-Ertrages aller Grundstücke normirt, so würde sie gegenwärtig 5 Procent des jetzigen Rein-Ertrags der Grundstücke und also, da der jetzige Rein-Ertrag der

Grundstücke in den meisten Provinzen das Dreifache, überall aber mindestens das Doppelte des Ertrags des Jahres 1815 ausmacht, mindestens noch einmal so viel als im Jahre 1815 betragen. Diese Erhöhung der Grundsteuer wurde allmälig eingetreten und daher durchaus nicht drückend für die Grundbesitzer gewesen sein. So aber bringt die Grundsteuer dem Staate jetzt nicht mehr ein, als sie im Jahre 1815 einbrachte, während alle andern directen und indirecten Steuern seit jener Zeit, wie dies bei dem gestiegenen Reichthum und bei der Vermehrung der Bevölkerung von 10 Millionen auf 18 Millionen Seelen nicht anders sein kann, ihren Ertrag verdoppelt haben.

Die jetzige Form der Grundsteuer hat daher wesentlich dahin geführt, daß trotz der Erhöhung fast aller übrigen Steuern und der in den letzten Jahren erfolgten Einführung einer neuen Steuer, der Einkommensteuer, und trotz des langen Friedens gegenwärtig die Finanzlage des Staates eine schlechte ist. Das Gleichgewicht zwischen Einnahmen und Ausgaben hat nur dadurch erhalten werden können, daß die Ausgaben für die Kriegsmarine, obwohl man deren Nothwendigkeit für die äußere Machtstellung Preußens schon seit mehr als einem Jahrzehend erkannt hat, lediglich aus finanziellen Rücksichten bis jetzt auf's Aeußerste beschränkt sind, und daß man fast sämmtlichen Staats-Beamten durchaus unzulängliche Gehalte gegeben hat.

§. 62.

Auf diesen letztern Punkt müssen wir näher eingehen, denn ohne genügende Gehalte ist es offenbar auf die Dauer unmöglich einen tüchtigen Beamten-Stand zu haben; von der Tüchtigkeit der Beamten hängt aber wesentlich die Handhabung der Gesetze ab.

Die Sachlage ist nun in dieser Beziehung folgende:

Die Besoldungen der Civil- und Militair-Beamten wurden fast sämmtlich in den Jahren 1815 und 1816 normirt, als die Nation durch den Krieg erschöpft war und der Staat sich in der drückendsten Finanznoth befand. Im Jahre 1825 wurden sie aus finanziellen Gründen erheblich herabgesetzt. In Folge der gestiegenen

Preise der Lebensmittel, Wohnungen und aller sonstigen Bedürfnisse sind nun aber Gehalte, die im Jahre 1816 ausreichend sein mochten, jetzt völlig unzulänglich geworden. Sowie es nun schon für einen Privatmann unehrenhaft ist, die in seinem Dienst stehenden Verwalter oder Fabrik-Aufseher so kärglich zu besolden, daß sie von ihrem Gehalte nicht leben können, so ist dies noch mehr hinsichtlich des Staats der Fall. Die schlechte pecuniäre Lage der Preußischen Beamten hat aber auch nicht ohne Einfluß auf deren Amts-Thätigkeit bleiben können. Die höhern Beamten zwar haben den Ruhm der Unbestechlichkeit, der noch vor 20 Jahren der Stolz unserer Nation war, bis jetzt behauptet. Anders ist es jedoch leider mit den Subaltern-Beamten. Was z. B. die Postbeamten betrifft, so ward erst kürzlich in den Kammern von einem Vertreter des Ministerii officiell anerkannt, daß im Jahre 1859 von 5900 Beamten nicht weniger als 95, also auf 60 Beamten einer wegen Malversation entlassen ist!

Man kann im Durchschnitt annehmen, daß binnen einem Jahre von 30 Beamten einer durch Tod oder in Folge von Pensionirung abgeht; wenn nun aber von 60 Beamten durchschnittlich einer wegen Malversation cassirt werden muß, so ist im Postfache die Zahl der Beamten, die wegen erwiesener Unredlichkeit cassirt werden, fast halb so groß, als die der durch Tod oder in Folge von Altersschwäche abgehenden.

Leider verhält es sich auch in den andern Zweigen des Staatsdienstes mit der Unbestechlichkeit und Redlichkeit der Subaltern-Beamten nicht viel anders als im Postfache:

Wir wollen hier nur eine Thatsache anführen, die bereits mehrfach in den Zeitungen besprochen ist. Bei Gelegenheit eines Preßprozesses vor etwa 3 Jahren in Berlin ward vom Angeklagten, welcher der Beleidigung von Executoren im Amte beschuldigt war, behauptet und durch den aufgenommenen Beweis nachgewiesen, daß in Berlin bei gerichtlichen Executions-Vollstreckungen die Annahme von ungesetzlichen Geschenken Seitens der Executoren Jahre lang fast regelmäßig geschehen ist. Es ward namentlich durch zwei

Apotheker bekundet, daß sie längere Zeit hindurch im Auftrage des Vereins sämmlicher Apotheker Berlins die gerichtliche Einziehung von deren Gebühren bewirkt und dabei jährlich einige Tausend Executionen hätten vollstrecken lassen; hierbei sei es Regel gewesen, dem Executor, so oft eine Execution von Erfolg gewesen sei, ein Douceur zu geben. Wenn solche Thatsachen in Berlin unter den Augen der höchsten Staatsbehörden vor sich gehn, so brauchen wir nicht zu fragen, was in den Provinzen geschieht. Unmöglich aber hätte eine solche Jahre lang fortgesetzte Uebertretung der Gesetze Seitens der Berliner Gerichts-Executoren ungestraft bleiben können, wenn nicht ein großer Theil der Gerichts-Boten und Executoren in einer solchen Lage wären, daß sie, um mit ihren Familien leben zu können, zu ungesetzlichen Nebenverdiensten greifen müssen.

Will der Staat wieder die frühere Ehrenhaftigkeit der Subaltern-Beamten herstellen, so bleibt ihm Nichts übrig, als das Mittel zu ergreifen, welches in den letzten Jahren in den meisten kleinern Staaten Deutschlands angewendet ist, nämlich eine angemessene Gehalts-Erhöhung. Schon der Gerechtigkeit wegen dürfte diese aber nicht bloß auf die Subaltern-Beamten beschränkt bleiben, da viele von den sogenannten höhern Beamten, z. B. die Mitglieder der Kreisgerichte, Regierungs-Assessoren u. s. w. pecuniär verhältnißmäßig noch schlechter als die Subaltern-Beamten gestellt sind. Sie müßte also auf fast alle Klassen der Civil- und Militair-Beamten ausgedehnt werden.

Daß eine solche Gehalts-Erhöhung nicht ohne den Aufwand von einigen Millionen jährlich zu bewirken ist, ist richtig; allein so schwer ein solches pecuniäres Opfer auch an sich sein mag, so darf man dasselbe doch nicht scheuen, sobald es nothwendig ist, um dem Staate einen ehrenhaften und tüchtigen Beamtenstand und damit zugleich die beste Garantie einer gewissenhaften Handhabung der Gesetze zu sichern. So lange Preußen eine unumschränkte Monarchie war, bestand fast die einzige Garantie für die Beobachtung der Gesetze, abgesehen von der Persönlichkeit des Königs, in der Ehrenhaftigkeit der Beamten.

Die jetzt herrschende Preßfreiheit und die parlamentarische Regierungsform haben zu dieser Garantie noch andere hinzugefügt, dürften aber schwerlich geeignet sein, jene erste Garantie entbehrlich zu machen.

Der noch vor zwanzig Jahren stattfindende übermäßige Andrang zum Beamtenstande, namentlich zur juristischen Laufbahn, hat gegenwärtig aufgehört.

Die strebsamsten jungen Kräfte ziehn es vor, sich der industriellen Thätigkeit und den wissenschaftlichen Fächern, die mit dieser zusammenhängen, z. B. dem Bergfache, der Chemie u. s. w. zu widmen.

So erfreulich nun auf der einen Seite die Zunahme der Industrie ist, so ist doch auf der andern Seite zu wünschen, daß das Ueberhandnehmen derselben nicht auf Kosten des wissenschaftlichen und militairischen Geistes geschehe, der bisher den Ruhm unseres Vaterlands ausmachte. Nichts aber muß mehr dazu beitragen, die Achtung vor wissenschaftlichen Bestrebungen herabzusetzen, als die unehrenhafte Art, mit welcher der Staat im Allgemeinen gegenwärtig die Dienste derer, welche ihm ihre Kräfte widmen, seiner Beamten, belohnt.

§. 63.

Wenden wir aber von diesem augenblicklichen Uebelstande unsern Blick ab auf das Ganze der Entwickelung unserer Verfassung und Gesetzgebung seit der Zeit des großen Kurfürsten bis jetzt, so sehen wir, wie die Verfassung unter dem großen Kurfürsten aus einer aristokratisch-ständischen eine factisch völlig absolute Monarchie wird, in welcher bloß der Regent und seine Beamten über die Interessen der Nation entscheiden; wir sehn, wie seit der Zeit der Befreiungskriege sich das Bedürfniß nach einer größern Betheiligung der Nation an öffentlichen Angelegenheiten geltend macht und zur Verleihung der Verfassung vom 30. Januar 1850 führt, welche nicht bloß einzelne bevorrechtete Stände, sondern die ganze Nation zur Theilnahme an politischen Rechten beruft; wir sehn ferner, wie die Gesetzgebung unter der Regierung des großen Kurfürsten zwar sämmtliche aus dem Mittelalter stammende Stände-Vorrechte und eine der Leibeigenschaft verwandte Abhängigkeit des Bauernstandes beibehält, wie jedoch seit der Regierung des Königs Friedrich I. durch eine verbesserte Armenpflege und zugleich durch zahlreiche Edicte, welche den Schutz der Gutsunterthanen gegen Bedrückung bezweckten, allmälig die sociale Stellung der niedern Stände verbessert wurde, bis das Edict vom 9. October 1807 eine fast vollständige Rechtsgleichheit aller Staatsbürger herbeiführte; wir sehn endlich, daß die Gesetzgebung der Verbesserung und Weiterbildung des Civil- und Criminal-Justiz-Verfahrens eine fast unausgesetzte Theilnahme schenkte, daß Preußen namentlich durch frühzeitiges Verbot der Hexenprozesse, Abschaffung der Tortur und Milderung der Strafgesetze, und durch Einführung eines vollständigen Gesetzbuchs im vorigen Jahrhundert, sowie durch Einführung des öffentlichen und mündlichen Gerichts-Verfahrens und der Geschwornen-Gerichte während der letzten Jahrzehnde den meisten andern Deutschen Staaten voranging, während in Handhabung der Gesetze und Verwaltung des Staats der Beamten-Stand, wenn wir von den traurigen Erscheinungen absehn, die in dem letzten Jahrzehend durch die ungenügende Besoldung der Subaltern-Beamten herbeigeführt sind, eine seltene Treue und Uneigennützigkeit zeigte.

Große Aufgaben sind es, deren Lösung die Nation von der Gesetzgebung der nächsten Jahre erwartet. Es gilt vor Allem, die Gemeinde-, Kreis- und Provinzial-Ordnung der östlichen Provinzen den jetzigen socialen Verhältnissen und den Principien der Verfassung gemäß umzuformen und zugleich dem ganzen Staate ein einheitliches Civilgesetzbuch zu geben.

Möge unsere Gesetzgebung die ihr obliegende Aufgabe in würdiger Weise lösen, möge sie auch in der Zukunft eine solche sein, daß sie dem übrigen Deutschland als Muster dienen könne und daß sie der geistigen und wissenschaftlichen Bildung, deren unsere Nation mit Recht sich rühmen kann, nicht unwerth sei.

CPSIA information can be obtained
at www.ICGtesting.com
Printed in the USA
LVHW040148220423
745008LV00001B/62

9 783112 382592